CRITICAL CHOICES

CRITICAL CHOICES

THE UNITED NATIONS, NETWORKS, AND THE FUTURE OF GLOBAL GOVERNANCE

WOLFGANG H. REINICKE
AND FRANCIS DENG

with

JAN MARTIN WITTE,
THORSTEN BENNER,
BETH WHITAKER,
AND JOHN GERSHMAN

INTERNATIONAL DEVELOPMENT RESEARCH CENTRE
Ottawa · Cairo · Dakar · Johannesburg · Montevideo · Nairobi · New Delhi · Singapore

Published by the International Development Research Centre
PO Box 8500, Ottawa, ON, Canada K1G 3H9
http://www.idrc.ca

© Better World Fund, United Nations Foundation 2000

Canadian Cataloguing in Publication Data

Reinicke, Wolfgang H.

Critical choices : the United Nations, networks, and the future of global
governance

Includes bibliographical references.

ISBN 0-88936-921-6

1.   United Nations.
2.   International organization.
3.   International cooperation.
I.   Deng, Francis Mading, 1938-   .
II. Witte, Jan Martin.
III. International Development Research Centre (Canada)

JX1977.C74 2000   341.23   C00-980198-7

IDRC Books endeavours to produce environmentally friendly publications.
All paper used is recycled as well as recyclable. All inks and coatings are
vegetable-based products.

CONTENTS

FOREWORD

Our world is getting smaller. Political and economic liberalization, together with sweeping technological change, have made all of humanity more interdependent. New and exciting opportunities are emerging, as are new risks and new challenges. Undoubtedly, globalization has emerged as the key governance challenge for the 21st century, and making globalization sustainable will require creative new forms of cooperation by all sectors of our society.

This report is a major contribution to the ongoing debate on globalization and governance. It goes beyond the merely theoretical by presenting one practical and promising avenue to address governance challenges: global public-policy (GPP) networks. In these networks, states, international organizations, civil society, and the corporate sector collaborate to make globalization work for all.

Over its 30-year history, Canada's International Development Research Centre (IDRC) has helped to establish many such networks. IDRC's experience in facilitating, through research and policy networks, South–South and South–North collaboration truly exhibits that the sum is often greater that its constituent parts. Take, for example, the Crucible Group. Supported by IDRC, the Canadian International Development Agency, and a number of other international organizations, the Group includes members from private industry, government, advocacy groups, and aboriginal groups. Since 1993 it has provided a forum for serious debate and policy recommendations on intellectual property rights, biodiversity, and food security.

Building on existing knowledge, the authors of *Critical Choices* explore both the promise and the limits of GPP networks. They present hands-on practical advice on the design, implementation, and promotion of GPP networks and explore how this new form of cooperation could help address the risks and opportunities presented by globalization.

In our globalizing world, the United Nations needs to find ways to collaborate with civil society and the global business community in tackling the challenges that lie ahead. By promoting GPP networks, the United Nations will more effectively serve its member states and fulfill its mission to address the problems of humanity. It is our task to make these networks work for all, in both North and South.

Maureen O'Neil
President
International Development Research Centre

PREFACE

The UN Vision Project on Global Public Policy (GPP) Networks was launched in early July 1999 in Washington, DC. In the following 5 months, the project team worked on numerous activities in addition to this report. The GPP website has been developed into an important tool for advertising project activities and obtaining important information and other inputs for the project. It allowed an electronic dialogue to be launched on topics pertinent to the GPP theme. The project held several workshops and seminars in Washington in cooperation with the United Nations Strategic Planning Unit, the United Nations Development Programme, and the World Bank. A number of publications were completed during the project's duration, and team members prepared briefings for policymakers; members of the business, academic, and policy communities; activists; and foundations (see various appendixes). The GPP theme featured in several speeches and keynote addresses at meetings and conferences in the United States and abroad. Finally, the project was able to attract additional funding from several foundations, which was critical to the team's ability to deliver on these activities and others to be conducted over the next several months. More information can be found on the GPP website (www.globalpublicpolicy.net).

The UN Vision Project on Global Public Policy Networks relied on the principles of network-building. Christina Bishop, Sören Buttkereit, and Travis Creighton supported the many additional activities that the project undertook, and David Earnest designed and managed the website. Their effort and dedication lie at the heart of this project. We are also grateful to our case-study authors, who, in most cases on short notice, each provided us with an analysis of a particular network of interest (see Appendix 2 for a list). Numerous colleagues provided valuable comments on the design of the project and drafts of the report. They include Monica Baker, Amy Batson, Ron Berenbeim, John Briscoe, Michael Edwards, Mohamed El-Ashry, Hansjörg Elshorst, Jean-Claude Faby, Curtis Farrar, Michael Feller, Martha Finnemore, Hilary French, Harald Fuhr, Ashraf Ghani, Branislav Gosovic, Geeta Rao Gupta, Ernst B.

Haas, Astrid Harnisch, Richard Higgot, Paul Isenman, Jacqueline
Kaiko, Barbara Kohnen, R. Andreas Krämer, Ralf Juan Leiteritz,
Carlos Lozada, Edward Luck, Kamal Malhotra, Hanns W. Maull,
Cord Meier-Klodt, Jennifer Mitchell, Jennifer Mosley, Andreas
Obser, Cornelia Quennet-Thielen, Thomas Risse, Frank Rittner,
James N. Rosenau, Edward Peter Russell, Charles Sabel, Arshad
Sayed, Hans-Peter Schipulle, Susan Sechler, Kathryn Sikkink,
John Steinbruner, Achim Steiner, John Stremlau, Maurice Strong,
Raimo Vayrynen, Joe L. Washington, Steven Weber, Hans-Heinrich
Wrede, and Michael Zürn, as well as the participants in our three
workshops. Michael Treadway edited the report and drafted the
executive summary.

We are grateful to the members of our advisory board for their
support of the project. Wolfgang H. Reinicke would like to thank
James D. Wolfensohn, President of the World Bank, for granting
him a partial secondment from his duties at the World Bank for the
duration of the project. We also gratefully acknowledge the support
of the United Nations Foundation, the Rockefeller Foundation, the
Fritz Thyssen Foundation, and the Hoechst Foundation.

EXECUTIVE SUMMARY

Profound and continuing change in our global environment —
social, political, and economic — today demands commensurate
changes in our institutions of global governance, not least in the
institution that lies at the core of the international system, the
United Nations. The organization faces a series of critical choices
in responding to these fundamental challenges. Creative new
arrangements are needed urgently to allow governments, other
organizations, both public and private, and individuals around the
world to work together to address pressing global problems — from
weapons control, to the lack of adequate global labour standards, to
climate change — as they arise. This report examines one such set of
arrangements: global public-policy (GPP) networks.

Having developed in the shadow of traditional multilateralism, GPP
networks are protean things, difficult to define or typologize. This
is so precisely because they have grown up largely independently of
each other to serve widely differing purposes. They do, however,
have a few things in common. One common denominator is that
they link together interested individuals and institutions not only
from diverse countries but also from diverse sectors of activity:
local, national, and regional governments; transnational corporations and other businesses and their associations; and what has
come to be called civil society. They thus cut cleanly across the fault
lines between various sectors, existing organizations, and sovereign
territories. Another commonality is that all these networks have
made intense and often ingenious use of the new information
technologies that for several decades have been transforming our
workplaces, our markets, and many of our other social institutions.
These "trisectoral" networks have already proved themselves to be
effective, often remarkably so, in bringing together diverse and
sometimes opposing groups to discuss common problems that no
one of them can resolve by itself; and in marshaling resources —
intellectual, financial, physical — to bring to bear on those
problems.

ORIGINS AND OBJECTIVES

Broadly speaking, GPP networks emerged as a response to two dynamic forces that took shape and spread throughout the world in the late 20th century. The first is **liberalization**, both economic and political. Economic liberalization, by opening markets, increasing competition, and encouraging the spread of capital, skills, and know-how worldwide, promises to raise standards of living in those countries that have embraced it. But the rapid dismantling of barriers to trade and capital flows has also had negative spillover effects, of which the recent financial crises in East Asia, Latin America, and the Russian Federation are prominent examples. At the same time, political liberalization in many countries has brought greater democracy to millions who long yearned for it, but it has also brought greater complexity to political and social issues and interactions.

The second broad force driving change is the **technological revolution**, and in particular the revolution in information technology. Technological change, too, has had immensely beneficial effects on the way we interact in commerce, public affairs, and society. But it has also made social, cultural, and economic relations far more complex and intertwined — and harder to predict and stabilize — and the pace of that change has clearly outstripped the ability of governments to manage the rapid consequences of the succession of technological advances.

The negative effects of these two sweeping forces on institutions of global governance may be characterized in terms of two governance gaps. First, an **operational gap** has opened up wherever policymakers and public institutions have simply found themselves lacking the information, knowledge, and tools they need to respond to the daunting complexity of policy issues in a liberalizing, technologizing, globalizing world. Second, but related to the first, a **participatory gap** has manifested itself as this same increasing complexity thwarts common understanding of, and therefore agreement on, critical policy issues. This has sometimes led policymakers, intentionally or not, to exclude the general public or particular stakeholders from their deliberations.

GPP networks have lately emerged as a "growth industry," precisely as a way of bridging these gaps. GPP networks are learning organizations. Their broad membership allows them to tap information and expertise from a variety of backgrounds, thus providing a more complete picture of particular policy issues and giving voice to previously unheard groups. These networks are meant to complement public-policy institutions, not replace them. They help governments and multilateral agencies manage risks, take advantage of opportunities presented by technological change, be more responsive to their constituents, and promote change within bureaucracies.

A RANGE OF ACTIVITIES

GPP networks address governance gaps by performing a variety of diverse functions. This report highlights six of the most important of these, although, again, no simple typology can do justice to the full range of network activities. Most of the networks perform several of these activities, but each network does not necessarily perform all or even most of them:

↳ GPP networks get involved in **placing new issues on the global agenda** or raising the prominence of issues that have been neglected. All such networks do this to some degree, but one type of network — what has been called a transnational advocacy network — makes global consciousness-raising its primary objective. Advocacy networks often excel at making strategic use of the media and influential individuals. They typically articulate clear and narrowly focused goals for their activities and frame their chosen issue in a way that will have maximum impact, often by couching it in the language of a moral imperative. The International Campaign to Ban Landmines is a model of a global network that concentrated on a single issue and waged a successful media campaign to raise awareness of the problem and move toward its resolution.

↳ GPP networks facilitate the **negotiating and setting of global standards.** This is happening in areas as diverse as financial regulation and environmental management. Whereas agenda-setting often can be accomplished by a relatively few dedicated individuals, the complexity of negotiating and setting standards, as well as concerns of fairness and equity, typically requires the involvement of stakeholders from all sectors on a representative basis. Trisectoral networks can help overcome stalemates in highly conflict-ridden policy arenas. The World Commission on Dams (WCD) is a prototypical example: this network has managed to break the deadlock among development planners, contractors, and environmental groups over the building of large dams. It shows what can be accomplished with a truly trisectoral structure in terms of both membership and funding. Through case studies, a review process, and various consultations, the WCD aims to assist future decision-making on the planning, design, monitoring, and operation of large dams.

↜ Networks are natural mechanisms for **gathering and disseminating knowledge,** and some GPP networks make this their principal activity. The information technology revolution allows all kinds of knowledge, technical and nontechnical, to be shared without regard for distance or borders and at ever-lower cost. Networks that focus on this kind of activity tend to be especially successful when they link participants with access to various knowledge bases and when all participants are willing to rethink their own ideas and practices — to learn and relearn as well as to teach. One of the oldest global networks, the Consultative Group on International Agricultural Research (CGIAR), has contributed enormously to the discovery and worldwide propagation of new crop strains and farming techniques. Yet this well-established network has shown the flexibility to expand its purview to issues of sustainable production systems and has adopted a strong poverty focus. CGIAR has also created new institutional forms to increase the participation of stakeholders from all three sectors and respond to other challenges.

↜ GPP networks may also have a commercial dimension — **making new markets** where they are lacking and **deepening markets** that are failing to fulfill their potential. Left to their own devices, markets sometimes fail to produce certain goods — public goods — that the broader public interest demands. GPP networks can help bridge this gap between demand and supply.

The Medicines for Malaria Venture, for example, is a global network that seeks to improve the economic incentives for pharmaceutical companies to develop badly needed new antimalarial vaccines. Networks, by providing links to other sources of both finance and information about best practice, are also helping a host of microlending enterprises in developing countries to improve and expand their operations.

ᦁ Some GPP networks are designed specifically as innovative **implementation mechanisms** for traditional intergovernmental treaties. The Global Environment Facility has increasingly turned to trisectoral networking to achieve its mission of funding and implementing worthy projects in the area of environmental protection.

Much of what networks accomplish through these five functions can be thought of as products in some sense — sounder standards, better information, more complete markets. But networks also improve the process by which all these products and others come into being, and in so doing they help **close the participatory gap,** the sixth function. The intangible outcomes of networks — such as greater trust between participants and the creation of a forum for raising and discussing other new issues — are often as important as the tangible ones, and they may endure even longer. Transparency International, for example, has not only scored significant successes in the fight against official corruption but also built coalitions of trust between very diverse actors in this sensitive issue area.

THE CARE AND TENDING OF NETWORKS

This description of GPP networks may foster the impression that networks sprout and grow almost naturally when the need for them arises and the circumstances are propitious. And sometimes, in a sense, they do. Networks are nothing if not situational and opportunistic. But that does not mean they do not need careful cultivation and nurturing. Managing a network requires skilful social entrepreneurship, flexibility, imagination, and the ability to learn on the fly.

Perhaps most important, those who would presume to manage a network must first understand that it is seldom they, the managers, who will develop the solution to the problem that the network was formed to address. More often it is the stakeholders themselves who find the answers. But network managers play several critical roles, including that of managing the tensions and conflicts that inevitably arise from a committed search among disparate parties for solutions to real problems, and doing so in a way that keeps the participants engaged. Some of the functions that might appear in a network manager's job description are listed below:

✦ *Getting the network off the ground* — The first task, of course, is getting the network up and running. Often it is the vision, dynamism, and resolve of one or a few individuals — like Kadar Asmal, in the case of the WCD, or US Secretary of Labor Robert Reich, with the Apparel Industry Partnership — that provide the spark for a new network. In other cases the needed leadership is institutional: an example is the World Health Organization's role in launching the Roll Back Malaria initiative. Would-be founders of a network must concentrate on getting the network dynamics right from the start, which means getting the right people on board and creating a common, shared vision. They must also make sure that participants recognize their dependence on each other and on innovative collective thinking to solve the problem at hand. The leaders must take pains not to allow the network to become too closely tied to themselves or another individual or institution; rather, they must be willing, even eager, to share power and to "lead from behind."

✦ *Balancing adequate consultation and goal delivery* — A second challenge is getting the process right while getting the product out the door. It is important to allow for extensive consultation and discussion, especially in the start-up phase and when the participants have heretofore been adversaries or competitors. This gives legitimacy to the network process — but it also risks delay in achieving the results that the participants and their constituencies demand. Networks can help keep their efforts on the rails by setting "milestones" against which to measure their progress. They can also sometimes engineer "easy wins" that help to satisfy their constituencies while allowing longer incubating work to proceed.

꞊ꞏ *Securing sustainable funding* — All networks, even the most ad hoc and ephemeral, absorb resources, and resources cost money. Therefore, ensuring adequate funding for the network's activities is an inescapable task for network managers. Also, the manner in which funding is obtained is vital for the network's credibility and sustainability. Often, support needs to be trisectoral in nature, rather than coming from a single donor or sector, although this is less important for some networks, such as those whose primary purpose is implementation.

꞊ꞏ *Maintaining the "structure" in structural informality* — Networks must avoid falling into the trap of becoming just another institution with an established bureaucracy and a rigid hierarchy. Network managers must therefore focus on maintaining "structured informality" — on keeping relationships loose and unconfining while building in enough organization and framework to get things done. One way to dodge the institutional trap is to build the network on existing institutions, keeping the network's own secretariat to a minimum. Built-in review processes, internal and external, can also help prevent ossification of the network's structures, practices, and people.

꞊ꞏ *Finding allies outside one's sector* — A useful strategy in fostering networks and their goals is to actively look for possible alliances across sectors. Sectors, after all, are not monolithic, and sometimes intrasectoral divides create opportunities for innovative intersectoral networking, where people and institutions in diverse sectors can find common ground.

꞊ꞏ *Tackling the dual challenge of inclusion* — Even in a world where political liberalization and technological change have made it far easier than before for people to connect, inclusion of all interested parties in a network's activities remains difficult. Much of a network manager's efforts relate to tackling the dual challenge of local–global and North–South inclusion, that is, bringing local interested parties into the global dialogue and bringing stakeholders in developing countries into a process that tends to be dominated by industrial-country elites. But inclusion is crucial to a network's legitimacy and accountability, as well as important on a normative basis. It is also a practical imperative: networks often need local people and institutions to implement their decisions on the ground. Networks have pursued various strategies to achieve greater inclusion. They can define and pursue multiple levels of engagement, for example by establishing organizations at the national level whose deliberations feed into the global network. They can establish structures that institutionalize inclusion, such as representative-voting arrangements and innovative funding mechanisms. They can build on existing initiatives and approaches, working from the bottom up. Or they can do the opposite, adapting global policies to fit local realities. Finally, networks can help build up the limited financial and organizational capacity of those local and developing-country actors whose inclusion they seek, such as by providing access to information technology, expertise, or direct funding.

WHAT ROLE FOR THE UNITED NATIONS?

The leadership of the United Nations has begun to place the idea of GPP networks at the forefront of its vision and strategy. In his 1999 address to the annual meeting of the World Economic Forum, UN Secretary-General Kofi Annan observed the following:

> The United Nations once dealt only with governments. By now we know that peace and prosperity cannot be achieved without partnerships involving governments, international organizations, the business community, and civil society.

This statement indicates a clear recognition that for the United Nations to succeed in its mission in the new millennium, it needs to develop a systematic and reliable approach to working with all sectors.

The Secretary General's Millennium Report — *We, the Peoples: The Role of the United Nations in the 21st Century*, in support of which this publication was written — points out the importance of global public policy networks in redefining the role of the UN:

> Formal institutional arrangements may often lack the scope, speed and informational capacity to keep up with the rapidly changing global agenda. Mobilizing the skills and other resources of diverse global actors, therefore,

may increasingly involve forming loose and temporary global policy networks that cut across national, institutional and disciplinary lines. The United Nations is well situated to nurture such informal "coalitions for change" across our various areas of responsibility.

By acting as a facilitator and platform for GPP networks, the United Nations can play an intermediary role between states, whose rationale and legitimacy for the foreseeable future will remain constrained by territorial sovereignty, and business and civil society, which, taking advantage of open markets and the technological revolution, have long escaped those constraints. By working with GPP networks and facilitating their emergence, the United Nations can help strengthen the capacities of state and nonstate actors to participate in the development of GPP while increasing its own effectiveness and credibility. In many ways, the future of GPP networks is the future of the United Nations, and vice versa.

The United Nations has been involved in many of the networks discussed in this report. However, it has yet to develop a strategic approach on how best to coordinate its efforts to engage in GPP networks. This report proposes a three-track approach that is both visionary and feasible:

✦ Strengthen and consolidate existing networks by focusing on implementation and learning processes;

✦ Build implementation networks that will help to revitalize weak or weakening conventions that are important to the UN's mission; and

✦ Launch new networks where they are needed.

To implement this three-track approach and decide on its own role in a strategic manner, the United Nations has to become more selective in its network involvement, on the basis of its own comparative advantages. As the case studies surveyed in the report show, the United Nations can play various roles at various times in GPP networks:

✦ The organization can act as convenor by, for example, organizing meetings on issues where conflicts occur across the North–South divide;

ᛒ UN agencies can act as providers of a platform and a safe space for negotiations and the development of consensual knowledge;

ᛒ Staff can act as social entrepreneurs, using the skilled leadership of top UN officials but also focusing on inclusion, effectiveness, and results at the operational level;

ᛒ UN agencies can act as norm entrepreneurs in such areas as sustainable human development, human rights, and disarmament;

ᛒ UN agencies can act as multilevel network managers by coordinating program activities or developing strategies for interacting with appropriate levels of governance;

ᛒ UN agencies can act as capacity-builders to ensure inclusiveness, both from a local–global and a North–South perspective; and

ᛒ Despite increasing difficulty, in some rare cases the United Nations can act as financier for operational programs.

The United Nations needs to develop mechanisms for the prioritization and coordination of those nascent issues that call for UN involvement. It also needs to ensure that its own activities neither duplicate the work of other multilateral organizations nor work at cross-purposes to them.

The Administrative Committee on Coordination and the United Nations Development Group are two venues within the UN system that could complement each other's activities to fulfill the many tasks that successful network management, including implementation, requires. In addition, a clearinghouse could be set up to act as an information hub for network activities, both within the United Nations and beyond. For the United Nations to become an active player in GPP networks, it needs to reach out to its external partners. One stepping-stone to improving relations and entering into a constructive strategic dialogue with key actors from nongovernmental organizations and the business community would be to develop the Global Compact on a trisectoral basis. By making itself a safe place for all the key actors to convene to negotiate politically controversial issues, the United Nations could fill a major gap in governance.

CONCLUSIONS

The United Nations faces a set of critical choices. The world organization needs to pay attention to its ability to offer itself as a safe place, not only for its traditional stakeholders — member governments — but also for the business community and civil society. Trisectoral networks provide the United Nations with a mechanism to rebuild its credibility and, indeed, the only way to achieve its increasingly complex missions with scarce resources in the 21st century. The organization's ability to effectively initiate, maintain, and participate in such networks will largely determine the extent to which it can achieve its mission — not least in the eyes of its constituents.

By successfully engaging in GPP networks, the United Nations performs a vital service to its member states. For it is they that are ultimately strengthened by these networks' activities. It is crucial for member states of the United Nations to understand that GPP networks are meant, not to replace governments, but to complement them. Networks help member states take advantage of the benefits and address the challenges of technological change and economic and social integration and thus perform their duties to their citizens in a more effective and legitimate way. GPP networks represent a unique opportunity for governments to regain the initiative in the debate over the future of global governance.

GPP networks embrace the very forces of globalization that have confounded and complicated traditional governance structures, challenging the operational capacity and democratic responsiveness of governments. They are distinctive in their ability to bring people and institutions from diverse backgrounds together, often when they have been working against one another for years. Making use of the strength of weak ties, networks can handle this diversity of actors precisely because of the productive tensions on which they rest. GPP networks do not offer an easy ride, but the difficulties are well worth the risk, given the daunting challenges of a complex world with an ever-expanding multiplicity of actors, interests, and issues to be resolved.

The stakes are high. Globalization is not, after all, the end of history. It is time to take a proactive stance lest we witness a full-fledged backlash against globalization. The status quo is unsustainable, and a change for the worse by forcing globalization back into national boundaries — "moving forward into the past" — is not an unlikely scenario. Networks can help to change this unsustainable status quo for the better, by responding to the challenges and taking full advantage of technological change and economic and social integration. Ultimately, it is up to the political will of the member states to endorse such a course of action. But it is the duty of the United Nations to lay out to its members the challenges that face them at the dawning of the new millennium and offer them an achievable agenda for meeting those challenges.

Chapter 1

INTRODUCTION

At the beginning of the 21st century, *globalization* has become the
term of choice to describe the changing external environment in
which all of us, individuals and institutions, now live and work. Yet,
so far at least, governments and international organizations have
fallen short in their efforts to develop mechanisms to allow their
citizens to take full advantage of the opportunities that globalization
offers. Nor have they succeeded in developing mechanisms that
effectively respond to the risks that a social and economic transformation of this scope entails. This report discusses a mechanism —
global public-policy (GPP) networks — that has the potential to
address both of these needs, and it considers their implications for
international organizations in general and the United Nations in
particular.

Two forces, by now familiar to us all, stand out as driving the change
in our international environment. First, for almost four decades
now, a general trend toward economic and political liberalization
has reshaped the international system. Economic liberalization has
opened markets, increased competition, and sharpened the international division of labour. For many years this development was
considered for the most part uncontroversial. But during the last
decade, the dismantling of economic barriers has been met with
growing apprehension, as transnational economic activity has generated a variety of negative spillover effects that governments and
international organizations have so far been unable to address in
a satisfactory manner. At the same time, many countries have been
undergoing a related but often conflict-ridden process of political
liberalization. This has fostered the growth of organizations representing what has come to be called civil society, and it has enabled
them to build transnational linkages and alliances. Meanwhile, both
political and economic liberalization have spurred the growth and
reach of transnational corporations, which today account for a substantial share of economic activity in many countries.

The changes wrought by economic and political liberalization have been sweeping. Yet even they have been superseded by the second force now reshaping the environment for international organizations. That force is the technological revolution, which already has brought lasting and profound changes to the world we live in. For governments in particular, technological change has transformed the way in which information and knowledge are created, processed, and disseminated; managing this flow of information constitutes the key challenge that public institutions face nowadays. Although technological advances may actually strengthen public institutions to some degree, their rapidity has clearly outstripped governments' ability to structure and make adequate use of them. Technological change has also made social, cultural, and economic relations more intertwined and more complex and inherently more difficult to predict or stabilize. The financial crisis that recently erupted in Asia and the debate about the appropriate social response to scientific advances in the genetic modification of organisms are two disparate but dramatic illustrations of what policymakers are up against. It is almost self-evident that deeper social and economic integration, coupled with the revolution in technology, requires that a growing number of "public goods" be provided at the global level. Less clear is whether the right structures and institutions now exist at the global level to facilitate such a process. After all, what is or is not in the public interest is not something that can be determined a priori. Rather, it is the outcome of the public-policy-making process, which in any system governed by democratic principles must be participatory and transparent and reflect the view of the majority of those affected.

Although many would argue that international institutions are the obvious and appropriate choice in facilitating such "global public-policy" processes, they are presently not adequately prepared for the task. In fact, the forces described above present direct and immediate challenges to the current architecture of global governance, at the core of which is the United Nations. The geographic reach and accelerated pace of economic and social activity, the growing recognition of the daunting complexity of many public-policy issues, and the acknowledgment that many issues must embrace a perspective on intergenerational equity have all created an **operational gap**, as policymakers and institutions often simply lack the information, knowledge, and tools to respond. In addition, political liberalization and technological change have opened a **participatory gap**, as individuals and private organizations increasingly perceive themselves as excluded from policy decision-making in their supposedly democratic institutions. Policymakers and international public institutions can no longer afford to bypass the concerns of the private sector and civil society, which have successfully politicized many global issues and have accumulated significant financial, ideological, and bargaining resources. There can be no doubt that the continuing inability of public institutions — states and international organizations alike — to address both these gaps will ultimately put their legitimacy at risk or provoke a backlash against liberalization and technological change. Indeed, there are clear signs that both are already starting to happen.

Today's global environment demands creative institutional arrangements to allow governments, other organizations, and individuals to agree upon and solve emerging global problems, whose number and intensity will only continue to grow. This report examines one such set of arrangements, which we call GPP networks. GPP networks are a means of responding to the uncertain and rapidly changing conditions of our relentlessly liberalizing and technologizing global environment. They address problems that defy disaggregation and parcelization among technocrats within a territorial hierarchy. Yet, like the global challenges they seek to address, the solutions they offer both reflect and embody the underlying forces of technological change and integration. GPP networks create bridges between the public sector — national, provincial, state, and local governments, as well as intergovernmental bodies — and the other two sectors of our society: the business community and civil society. These trisectoral networks have the potential to pull diverse groups and resources together and address issues that no one sector can resolve by itself. By no means are these networks only about "process" — to the contrary. As the case studies surveyed in this report show, they also deliver tangible outcomes — for example, extending credit to the poor, assisting countries facing environmental challenges, and fighting infectious diseases.

Many efforts made thus far to describe and analyze the structures and processes of global governance have tended to focus on more formal, established institutions and organizations. By concentrating on these old and well-worn stories, we may be missing a quiet revolution. Equating politics with political institutions masks a simple truth: individuals and groups, not bureaucracies or formal institutions, drive innovation and learning. Change is a bottom-up process, not a top-down steering committee. Until recently, only the most prominent and vocal networks, such as the International Campaign to Ban Landmines (ICBL), have caught the public's attention; others, such as the World Commission on Dams (WCD) and the Consultative Group on International Agricultural Research (CGIAR), are less well known. But there are already as many as 50–60 GPP networks in existence, ranging in focus from crime and pollution to fisheries and public health.

Their informal and often legally nonbinding character may partly explain why the story of GPP networks has gotten little attention. But until that story is told, policymakers must make do with little concrete information and knowledge about these organizations. What are their capacities? What are their limits? How do they differ from one another? Why do some succeed, and why do others fail? Can they (and should they) be "managed"? With so many networks in operation, can we yet discern best practices? And what role, if any, do they offer for international organizations, and the United Nations in particular, to play? These questions must be answered for GPP networks to attract the attention they deserve and demonstrate the value they can add.

In recent years, many scholars and policymakers have claimed that the increased role that corporate actors and nongovernmental organizations (NGOs) are playing in global politics undermines state capacity or the effectiveness of international organizations, especially the United Nations. However, this is not always the case. To the contrary, as this report shows, cooperation across different sectors often helps states and international organizations to live up to their commitments and fulfill their missions. One thing we can say is that the sheer variety of networks we encounter suggests that there is not yet a consistent pattern of network-building; they seem to develop differently according to their differing circumstances and conditions. Networks are nothing if not situational and opportunistic. This poses limits on how much this report can deliver in terms of systematic analysis, conclusions, and recommendations. For this reason, the report does not attempt to force all of these various networks into a rigid typology or structure for analysis. Indeed, the very nature of networks may make this an elusive goal. Rather, we take an inductive approach, scrutinizing and describing what is out there, trying to discern best practices, and pointing to some initial lessons learned — lessons that we hope will help maintain and strengthen existing networks and perhaps launch new ones to face the challenges ahead.

It is too early to determine the full potential of trisectoral networks — or their limits. We might well be in the early stages of a paradigm shift (to use Thomas Kuhn's now-familiar phrase) in global governance, the frontiers of which remain to be explored. As Kuhn reminds us, under these circumstances practice will inform theory and improve our understanding of how these networks tick and where they can be useful. Of course, networks are no panacea for the world's problems, but using them wisely will no doubt improve our ability to cope with the difficult challenges posed by rapid global liberalization, technological change, and the complexity these trends have brought to our lives.

Chapter 2 fleshes out our characterization of the two global forces transforming the world. These forces, often lumped together under the catch-all term *globalization*, are already quite familiar and require no detailed elaboration, and so we focus on their features that are relevant to later discussion. The chapter then considers the implications of this transformation and concludes that two gaps, operational and participatory, have emerged in global governance and have challenged national and international public institutions in a fundamental way.

Chapter 3 presents empirical evidence confirming the relevance of GPP networks in taking on the challenges identified in Chapter 2. After a brief overview of the foundations of network theory and its implications for the organization of global governance, we turn to an examination of what we regard as the core functions that networks perform. This examination is based on the case studies commissioned for this report. (Appendix 2 lists the case studies and their authors.) If managed in an effective and legitimate manner, GPP networks can indeed narrow the governance gaps.

Chapter 4 identifies several critical managerial issues common to almost all GPP networks and distils the lessons, positive and negative, that can be learned from existing cases. What is the role of leadership? How can networks best combine consultation and delivery? How can sustainable funding be ensured? How can networks meet the dual challenge of inclusion (North–South and local–global)?

Chapter 5 discusses what role there is for the United Nations, the only truly universal world organization, to play with respect to GPP networks. A review of the UN's experience with networks to date leaves little doubt that the organization can appropriately take on several critical functions in support of networking. But even as a changing global environment has made the UN's engagement in networks an attractive proposition, the organization's own future relevance and ability to deliver on its mission are by no means assured. Critical for the UN's success in GPP networks, and thus in global governance at large, will be its ability to define its role carefully and selectively. Such a process of prioritization will in part be driven by external forces, in particular by the fact that the United Nations is an intergovernmental organization serving the interests of its members. But it should also be driven by internal considerations, in particular an analysis of the institution's own organizational strengths and weaknesses. Mindful of the political and economic constraints the United Nations is facing, but with a view toward positioning the United Nations in a strategic manner, the chapter closes with some recommendations to enhance its role in the initiation, maintenance, and operation of GPP networks so as to maximize opportunities for expanding the organization's impact.

GPP networks are not a substitute for existing institutions of global governance. Rather, they are a complement. However, to succeed they will require adjustment — both organizational and behavioural — on the part of others: nonstate actors, such as corporations and NGOs, as well as state actors, such as governments and international organizations. The leaders of the United Nations and other intergovernmental organizations, such as the World Bank, are keenly aware of the promise that a greater reliance on networks holds. Knowing that their own future is at stake, these organizations have begun to embrace the network concept and call for institutional change. There should be no illusions, however: global public-policy-making through collaborative networks is likely to challenge deeply entrenched political, economic, and bureaucratic interests. Trisectoral networks call hierarchies and their principles into question. Although it seems reasonable to expect that policy-makers and bureaucrats will try for as long as possible to adjust by adding new structures or adopting new functions at the margin, a more genuine overhaul of their governance structures and activities may prove necessary in the long run. The United Nations thus faces a set of critical choices in the future that require creativity and leadership, both of which are usually in short supply. This report highlights some of these choices and hopes to offer strategic guidance.

Chapter 2

A CHANGING EXTERNAL ENVIRONMENT

What are the challenges to which GPP networks respond? What are the forces that drive their development? What underlying changes in the international system make GPP networks such a potentially useful tool to increase the effectiveness and efficiency of global governance? This chapter lays out the framework for our examination of GPP networks by analyzing the two momentous developments that today propel continuous change in the environment of our global public institutions: political and economic liberalization and technological change. Although both developments play a role in the emergence of what we call an **operational gap** in global governance, this chapter argues that they also cause a **participatory gap** that undermines the legitimacy of existing governance mechanisms: the state and the multilateral system. And though part of the challenge is technocratic, one should not underestimate the role of norms and values in creating those gaps — and in resolving them. After all, public-policy-making is a difficult process that involves conflict and the reconciliation of divergent interests.

Since the birth of the United Nations in 1945 the international system has undergone a dramatic transformation, which accelerated during the last decade. Policymakers, national and international alike, face a rapidly changing external environment. A broad wave of economic and political liberalization around the world, together with rapid technological advances, continues to generate profound challenges for public institutions and bureaucrats. The public sector's inability to adequately absorb and respond to these forces has led to two governance gaps that are evident in public-policy-making today.

The first of these gaps arises from the fact that a growing number of public-policy issues can no longer be effectively addressed in existing institutional frameworks, whether at the national or at the intergovernmental level. The increasing geographic reach and complexity of public-policy issues and the speed with which they arise and propagate make governance an ever more convoluted and

9

frustrating process. The resulting operational gap in governance is a serious challenge to public-policymakers.

The second gap is directly related to the first. As states and international organizations lose their credibility and legitimacy, in part because of the operational shortcomings just described, an acute participatory gap emerges in international governance. Private entities, in business and civil society, many of which have successfully reorganized themselves on the transnational level, now operate in a governance vacuum. They are acutely aware that no institutional framework now exists to adequately express and aggregate their interests and implement solutions to their problems in line with the most basic models of democratic governance. Although perhaps less glaring than the operational gap, this participatory gap is by no means less important, and it deserves equal attention and innovative thinking.

ECONOMIC AND POLITICAL LIBERALIZATION

For almost four decades now, a general trend of increasing economic and political liberalization has reshaped the international system. Economic liberalization has opened up markets and increased competition and the international division of labour. Following the principles of liberal internationalism, states have deliberately deregulated and liberalized their domestic economies, opening them to international trade and capital flows, including foreign direct investment (FDI). Private enterprises, taking advantage of this freer business environment, have spread their activities on a transnational and, indeed, increasingly global scale. We have not yet reached (and likely will never reach) the condition of a truly global market economy, where distance and boundaries dissolve into irrelevance. But production and consumption patterns are increasingly internationalized, creating new economic spaces that span multiple political geographies. Since the 1980s this emergence of transnational economic spaces has been largely driven by the organizational logic of corporate industrial networks and their financial relationships, which cut across national boundaries.

During the last decade, and particularly in the wake of the Asian financial crisis, this wholesale demolition of economic barriers has become more controversial, as transnational economic activity generates negative spillover effects that existing governance mechanisms have yet to effectively address. Less developed countries, in particular, are exposed to an ever-greater volatility and turbulence of global market forces, for which no equally global political framework provides shelter, order, and regulation. The postwar paradigm of "embedded liberalism" is no longer valid. Yet despite growing opposition, liberalization was given another push forward by the end of the Cold War, as Eastern Europe and the former Soviet Union chose to abolish their command economies and as countries in Africa and elsewhere overhauled their highly protective import substitution programs.

This process of economic liberalization has been accompanied in many countries by a process of political liberalization, related to, but more often beset by conflict than, its economic counterpart. Since the mid-1980s many countries in Africa, Eastern Europe, and Latin America have liberalized their domestic political systems, at times leading to the emergence of new sovereign states. The number of countries classified as electoral democracies by Freedom House increased from 69 in 1987 to 117 in 1998. This trend has had a number of important implications for the organization of governance in general and for notions of legitimacy and participation in public-policy-making in particular.

First, political liberalization has led in many countries to a proliferation of organizations of civil society and has, at the same time, enabled these organizations to form transnational alliances. According to the *Yearbook of International Organizations*, the number of international NGOs increased by more than 60% between 1981 and 1996. Some countries saw even more dramatic expansions. In sub-Saharan Africa, for example, it was not uncommon for the number of registered NGOs in a country to increase by as much as 400% within a decade. The trend was not limited to the developing world, however; countries like the United Kingdom and France also saw significant increases in the number of homegrown NGOs.

Second, with this growth and greater articulation of civil society, donor organizations have increasingly found it worthwhile to channel their support to their projects in developing countries through these NGOs, rather than through government agencies. In doing so, they see themselves as supporting democratization and assisting in the downsizing of overinflated state bureaucracies. It is estimated that NGOs disburse roughly 15% of all public development assistance worldwide and, in combination with other funding sources, deliver more than $10 billion (US currency throughout) worth of services and relief aid annually to the world's poorest people. International and local organizations of civil society have thus established direct relationships with donors in the industrialized world, and in turn the greater availability of donor funds to NGOs has inevitably contributed to the establishment of even more of these organizations. The result in many countries has been the emergence of a large civil-society sector with direct links to sources of international finance.

In similar fashion, the processes of political and economic liberalization have spurred the growth and reach of transnational corporations, which today account for a substantial share of economic activity in many countries. According to the UN's 1998 *World Investment Report*, in 1997 some 53 000 transnational companies controlled about 450 000 affiliated organizations worldwide. Sales of these companies amounted to $9.5 trillion in 1997, clearly outstripping all of world trade in that year. And just as international NGOs are heavily concentrated in the industrial countries, so, too, the overwhelming majority — some 90% — of transnational corporations are headquartered there.

The trend toward transnationalization of business activity and organization manifests itself in at least three ways. First, the rising incidence of cross-border mergers and acquisitions is a major driver of FDI flows and reflects companies' desire to divest noncore activities and build on their competitive advantages. Second, the growing significance of intrafirm trade reflects a restructuring of corporate activities, internalizing to the firm many cross-border economic activities that previously were conducted on the open market. Third, the number of interfirm alliances grew from fewer than 300 in the early 1980s to more than 600 in the mid-1990s. More than 8 200 interfirm agreements were concluded between 1980 and 1996.

These alliances mostly occur in high-technology and other knowledge-intensive industries, where firms join together in cross-national networks to share knowledge and information. These horizontal, interfirm networks allow the participating companies to source knowledge on a transnational scale and take advantage of economies of scale. Although the political significance of these transnational companies and their activities is still highly disputed, there can be no doubt that they play a very important role in economic development and have developed into key political players on the global stage.

In sum, countries have liberalized their political systems and economies and in the process allowed private actors — individuals and organizations — to play a greater role in determining public-policy outcomes. Civil society, NGOs, and businesses have come to play a greater role in economic development in many developing countries in recent years. Meanwhile, the successful liberalization of many domestic political systems has led to increased calls for the international system of governance to take a dose of the same medicine and to seek comparably constructive and fruitful ways to collaborate with business and civil society in global policy decisions.

The growth of national and transnational organizations of civil society has been especially important in increasing pressure on public institutions — states and international organizations alike — to open up and create new venues for access and political participation. At the domestic level, many of the traditional means (such as political parties) by which interests are aggregated and views conveyed to leaders have lost membership and public appeal. At the international level, organizations of civil society have emerged as important political players, successfully challenging international institutions to address their interests and concerns.

TECHNOLOGICAL CHANGE

Whereas the processes of economic and political liberalization have figured prominently in the interdependence debate since the late 1960s, more recently they have been superseded in importance by an ongoing technological revolution that has significantly changed the world in which we live. Technological change has transformed the way in which information and knowledge are created, processed, and disseminated, and this poses some difficult challenges for public institutions.

Technological change is in itself neither a curse nor a cure-all. It does both good and ill, usually both at once. On the one hand, advances in communications technologies have improved governments' ability to process information and knowledge. The activities of states and international organizations are becoming better coordinated and may yet culminate in what one observer calls an "international governmental information marketplace." On the other hand, technology often evolves faster than the social and regulatory environment in which it is embedded. As a result, social, cultural, and economic relations become more intertwined and inherently difficult to predict or stabilize.

The information technology revolution in general and the Internet in particular are good examples. New information technologies have enabled or facilitated many types of cross-border activity, which sometimes intrude on a government's capability to control economic and social relations within its territory. The Internet has doubtless improved the ability of public institutions to communicate, to share critical information, and to organize political and bureaucratic processes in a more efficient way. It has also helped NGOs, whose reach was formerly limited to a single locality or country, build powerful transnational coalitions. Business, too, has benefited from the rapid development of the Internet, which has created a whole new medium through which commerce can be pursued and the geographic reach of companies can be extended. These benefits notwithstanding, however, the public sector's inability to regulate information technology effectively has also led to some unfortunate spillover effects from the Internet. For example, the international drug trade increasingly organizes its distribution and payment systems by means of sophisticated e-mail and website systems. The Internet is an ideal instrument for organizing money-laundering, especially as the introduction of so-called e-money makes control even more complicated. The Internet has also facilitated the spread and sale of illegal pornographic material throughout the world. The proliferation of computer viruses and hackers seeking to manipulate critical computer systems poses serious risks to both the public and the private domain, and the threat will only grow in the future.

Falling costs of communication and coordination, driven by the information revolution, facilitate bottom-up organizing processes that strengthen nonstate actors, including businesses and NGOs. Both corporations and civil society have taught the public sector a lesson on this score: by relying on horizontal and flat organizational structures, rather than traditional hierarchies, they have gained power relative to governments and intergovernmental organizations that continue to operate on hierarchical principles. Horizontally organized entities have a distinct advantage over hierarchical ones in processing information and making use of knowledge in innovative ways.

More fundamentally, the transformation in the way in which information and knowledge are created, processed, and disseminated has made it more difficult for policymakers to control, structure, and use information and knowledge. Information and knowledge have always been a currency of power. But as many private companies have already learned over the past decade, their value has appreciated dramatically. Public policy has only begun to come to grips with the changing context. Technological change and speed, as well as the transparency by which information is processed, have an increasingly important impact not only on how we organize our lives as individuals but ultimately on social relations and political institutions as well. Taking a longer-term perspective, there is little doubt that technological change and the information revolution will radically transform the framework conditions within which policy is made.

THE MULTIDIMENSIONAL IMPACTS OF LIBERALIZATION AND TECHNOLOGICAL CHANGE

Although the implications of both technological change and liberalization can be felt at all levels of governance, as the discussion below demonstrates, the multiple dimensions of the problem are perhaps best seen at the global level.

THE GEOGRAPHIC DIMENSION AND THE TERRITORIALITY TRAP

It is now commonly accepted that with increasing social and economic integration, the geographic scope of public goods and bads extends far beyond national borders. For public-policymakers this has resulted in a dramatic information and knowledge gap between themselves and the nonstate social and economic networks that now span the globe. Governments struggle to respond to challenges about which they lack sufficient information and whose origin is far beyond their geographic reach (Box 1). Trapped by the territoriality of their power, they have little choice but to address the symptoms of public bads, rather than the causes. Nor are they likely, under present arrangements, to be able to preserve such public goods as health, a clean environment, and a safe and sound financial system in the future.

Box 1

Transnational collective action: the protection of the ozone layer

From the early 1970s on, scientific advocates stated that chlorofluorocarbons (CFCs) damaged the ozone layer. Although the scientific hypothesis that CFCs threatened to deplete stratospheric ozone immediately received widespread attention in the United States, other countries did not recognize the research as valid. The *Clean Air Act* of 1977 in the United States curtailed CFC production there but did not result in a reduction of CFC output worldwide, as European companies simply inherited the markets their US counterparts had lost. In addition, developing countries were increasingly producing and using the compounds.

CFC emission is a clear case of a global public bad, because many if not all countries around the world suffer its effects, at least in the long run, and because a successful response requires cooperation among a substantial number of countries, and especially the most important producers. Initial intergovernmental negotiations, however, failed to mobilize sufficient political support for the far-reaching measures so important for an effective worldwide reduction of CFC output. It took intensive lobbying by civil-society organizations, overwhelming scientific evidence, and some key events (in particular the discovery of the ozone hole over Antarctica in 1986), as well as the cooperation of key members of the business community, to bring about action. In 1987, 13 years after scientists had first explored the damaging effects of CFCs, states agreed under the Montreal Protocol to reduce worldwide CFC production by half.

THE TIME DIMENSION AND INTERGENERATIONAL EQUITY

If geography presents one set of constraints for policymakers, time presents another. As already indicated, the information revolution has dramatically reduced the ability of policymakers to respond to the changed condition of politics. The time that policymakers need to process, structure, and use knowledge so as to make informed decisions has become a scarce commodity, as 24-h media coverage of events from all around the world exerts unrelenting pressure to act, or rather react, quickly. The result is "instant politics," where far-reaching decisions are often made on the first available information. NGOs are often catalysts in these processes, building national and transnational advocacy coalitions to push policymakers to act in response to humanitarian crises or environmental disasters as soon as they arise.

More importantly, hierarchical bureaucratic structures often altogether lack the crucial information and knowledge base from which to make timely and effective public-policy decisions. The sheer speed with which complex technological change occurs alters the framework conditions of politics. Think, for example, about financial regulation or transnational crime. What we often observe is a recurring cycle of politicians losing grip on events, momentarily catching up, then once again falling behind, as if caught on a high-tech treadmill, constantly struggling to adapt to ever-changing external conditions. The effort to regulate international financial markets is a prime example (Box 2).

Perhaps most frustrating is the fact that even as the revolution in information technology has increased the premium on time, a growing number of public-policy issues — notably those focusing on the environment — require a perspective that spans generations. Decisions on environmental policy today will have implications for many generations to come. And it is far from clear whether a governance process driven by the political business cycle can cope with this gross mismatch between the time available for making decisions and the time over which our descendants will suffer the consequences (Box 3).

Box 2
Financial markets and the regulatory dialectic

Since the outbreak of the Latin American debt crisis, in 1982, the rising incidence of bank failure and growing systemic risk in the international financial system have become a matter of great concern for policymakers. In 1988, after enormous pressure from the United States, financial system regulators in the Group of Ten large industrial market economies agreed on the Basle Accord, which stipulates a one-size-fits-all capital adequacy standard for international banks.

However, by the time the final agreement on capital adequacy was announced in the summer of 1988, new challenges to the stability of the global financial system were already looming. As us Federal Reserve Board chair, Alan Greenspan, recently stated, other "deficiencies were [becoming] understood even as the Accord was being crafted." The industry quickly developed new financial instruments and business practices (involving securitization and derivatives trading) that effectively circumvent the standards. In addition, the emergence of internationally active financial conglomerates, embracing a range of different financial sectors (such as commercial and investment banking, as well as insurance), makes regulation increasingly complicated.

The resulting dynamic can be characterized as an ongoing regulatory dialectic. Every attempt on the part of public regulators to address dangers in the financial system is countered by rapid innovation by the financial services industry and the introduction of new financial instruments and business strategies. In this fast-changing environment, policymakers cannot react quickly enough to prevent gaps in regulatory coverage from emerging.

COMPLEXITY AND THE RISKS OF A PARTIAL VIEW

Even as they adjust to these ever more tightly binding constraints of geography and time, policymakers find themselves having to tackle more and more issues that cut across areas of bureaucratic or disciplinary expertise. Decisions made about international trade, for example, can have profound economic, ecological, and security effects, all of which must be considered in the policy debate. In essence, technological change and the information revolution have unleashed an increasing complexity on governance issues along two dimensions.

First, existing public-policy concerns are understood as increasingly difficult to define and as increasingly inseparable from other domains. Global policy decisions about the environment, as in the

Box 3
Forests and intergenerational equity

When it comes to the environment, our exploitative reach all too often exceeds our intellectual grasp. Tragically, much of the knowledge we need to gain a broader understanding of many environmental concerns and the complexity of ecosystems will only be acquired after our environment has been transformed and perhaps irreversibly damaged. This raises issues of intergenerational justice and equity, for knowledge about how to preserve ecosystems that have already been lost would be a bitter bequest to future generations.

Deforestation is a perfect example. Forests play a critical role in serving human needs. They are a prime source of water, food, protein, shelter, medicine, fodder, lumber, and soil, and they often provide a basis for tourism as well. Forests also stabilize landscapes and influence water flows, water quality, and the composition of the atmosphere. They are major reservoirs of biodiversity in all latitudes and home to various groups of indigenous people as well.

Yet almost half of the forests that once covered the Earth have been destroyed. Deforestation is occurring most rapidly in South America (especially the Amazon Basin), in Southeast Asia, and in Southern and Central Africa. An average of 15.4 million ha of forests of all types was lost each year during the 1980s — an area the size of Peru and Ecuador combined. The ultimate effects of deforestation not only on global climate change but also on myriad local ecologies and societies are still unknown. The greenhouse effect may yet drastically alter the Earth's climate, crippling economic development in both the developing and the developed world. Future generations will be confronted with this mounting and complex problem and will have to bear the burden of previous generations' disregard and lack of awareness.

Reforestation policies, along with a noticeable decrease in deforestation, would counter these effects, and international organizations are starting to answer the call. Funding of forestry preservation programs by the United Nations Development Programme, the United Nations Environment Programme, the World Bank, and related agencies grew substantially during the past decade. But although this greater emphasis on forest protection on the part of international agencies is a step in the right direction, trisectoral participation that emphasizes an intergenerational perspective will be imperative for success. It is true that the Intergovernmental Panel on Forests (IPF) and its successor, the Intergovernmental Forum on Forests (IFF), increasingly include other actors (NGOs and parts of the business community) in their consultation processes. So far, however, the IPF–IFF processes have failed to act as a forum for successful cooperation between actors from the various sectors and from Northern and Southern countries. Future forest management initiatives (such as the United Nations Forum on Forests) will have to strengthen both the trisectoral dimension and the link back to initiatives at the regional and local levels.

forests case discussed in Box 3, or about public health, such as how to control AIDS and malaria, have social, ecological, economic, and security repercussions, none of which can be simply ignored. This broadening of the problem domain challenges the knowledge and information base of national bureaucracies and their structures yet again.

Second, entirely new and complex problems have emerged that have not yet been fully understood. A case in point is the issue of how to pursue the potential benefits of genetic engineering for food security while minimizing the risks (Box 4). Because of the accelerating pace of technological change and the fact that states are increasingly linked into highly complex webs of political, social, economic, and environmental interdependencies, attempts to find feasible solutions for the world's problems need to be informed by systematic knowledge about the issue at hand, the circumstances, the relevant actors, and possible strategies. Getting the full picture becomes more and more of a problem for bureaucracies, not least because of the potential for myriad unintended consequences. The risk of a partial view, in turn, is growing higher and higher precisely because of the systemic consequences of decisions.

Box 4
Who will regulate genetic engineering?

The successful manipulation of plant and animal genes to enhance a variety of agricultural products has rapidly accelerated since the mid-1980s. Most of the research and development has taken place in the industrialized world in the private sector. Large chemical companies and agribusiness firms have discovered that these genetic alterations can dramatically increase the output of products such as wheat, rice, and milk while increasing their nutritional value. Both the products and the technologies developed are subject to mechanisms to protect intellectual property rights, such as patents. Disputes over the safety of these products threaten to disrupt agricultural trade between the United States and Europe.

Research and development of transgenic plants has focused on crops, cropping conditions, and markets of the industrialized countries and, to a lesser extent, of large-scale farms in higher income developing countries. About 75% of the area sown to transgenic crops is located in the United States and is mainly for maize, cotton, soybeans, and canola.

(continued)

Box 4 *concluded*

Poor farmers and consumers in developing countries would stand to benefit from the use of genetic engineering to develop drought- and pest-tolerant varieties of locally consumed food crops, such as cassava, millet, sorghum, rice, potatoes, and sweet potatoes. There is also potential to enhance the nutritional value of the foods consumed by poor people, perhaps providing an important means to address micronutrient malnutrition, which affects more than 2 billion people worldwide. However, in the absence of broader public-sector involvement, little research and development that is relevant to poor farmers and consumers will occur, as the private sector does not expect an attractive return on such work.

The regulation of transgenic crops involves many issues, including the following:

~ Biosafety — to prevent environmental risks, such as loss of biodiversity, collateral harm to beneficial species, and the drift of various genetic traits from food crops to their wild and weedy relatives, creating "superweeds";

~ Public health and food safety — to prevent the transfer of allergens and carcinogens through genetic engineering;

~ The possibility of monopoly profits; and

~ Intellectual property rights — to balance these against the right of farmers to save and replant seeds and the right of nations and communities to benefit equitably from their genetic resources.

Some of these issues are both unresolved and controversial. Developing countries lack the administrative capacity to implement regulations, even after the need has been determined. Regulatory capacity is also weak at the global level, where there is a lack of common understanding of the potential risks and benefits of genetic engineering and no appropriate institutional framework in which regulation could be negotiated. The Cartagena Protocol on Biosafety, on which 130 governments agreed in January 2000, is only a first step in the direction of regulating genetic engineering.

There is also growing concern that genetically altered organisms present an unprecedented threat to the global environment and to the health of the world's population. Many scientists argue that the unregulated use of these items could unleash an uncontrollable genetic chain reaction that would irreversibly alter the composition of various species. Currently, no international standards regulate the use of these materials, and consumer awareness through the use of labeling has been successfully thwarted by the lobbying strength of various large companies. The situation is worsened by a lack of communication between the companies performing the research and development and the developing nations that perceive themselves as threatened. Even now, we lack a common understanding of the potentials and risks of genetic engineering. In his Millennium Report, the UN Secretary General calls for a global public policy network to address the risks and opportunities associated with the increased use of biotechnology and bioengineering.

Together, geography, time, and complexity have created an operational gap that, if it persists as a governance gap, will cast doubt on the feasibility of democratic institutions. It is already an important factor in the declining trust in these institutions, and it is one to which governments and international organizations must respond.

To the extent governments cannot close the operational gap, the effectiveness of democracy itself is threatened. Citizens may continue to exercise their right to vote, yet the actual power of that vote to shape public policy decreases with the decline of the government's capacity to govern effectively within its borders. The same holds at the global level: international organizations that can no longer fulfill their mandates will have increasing difficulty justifying their existence.

THE PARTICIPATORY GAP

Even as these problems related to geography, time, and complexity contribute to an operational gap in governance and put the legitimacy of our democratic institutions at risk, political liberalization and technological change are also fueling a participatory gap that looms ever wider. States and international organizations can no longer afford to bypass the concerns of transnational actors who have successfully politicized many global issues and have strengthened their bargaining positions with significant financial and ideological resources. For example, NGOs have been very successful in placing the distributional aspects of economic integration and technological change on the global agenda and keeping them there. Transnational corporations, likewise, are increasingly important players and have gained political leverage relative to states and international organizations.

Yet, existing institutional processes and structures of governance offer these forces few points of access and active participation in public-policy-making. The United Nations and the World Bank have each made informal efforts to include both civil society and the private sector, but these clearly fall short of a concerted approach to bringing all sectors together and therefore may even be counterproductive (see Chapter 5). The formal governance structures of intergovernmental institutions have not changed at all. As already indicated, there are no transmission mechanisms by which the interests of scattered stakeholders can be aggregated and fed into the global political process. There is no global public space in which substantive discussion of transnational challenges can effectively take place and be acted upon in an open and participatory fashion. In fact, as long as there is no democratically structured institutional context, the often-cited "power shift" does indeed remain a zero-sum game. Without that context, the enhanced governance role of businesses and civil society cannot be fully translated into democratic decisions that strengthen the legitimacy of states and international organizations, turning today's zero-sum game into a positive-sum game. Creating an institutional framework in which those interests can be adequately represented and integrated into public-policy-making defines the challenge that GPP networks are designed to address (see Chapter 3).

This concern about participatory forms of governance highlights another important point. A purely technocratic view of the management of globalization, relying on efficiency and effectiveness as the only benchmarks, would be overly simplistic and neglect the role of norms and values. It is possible to focus too narrowly on the theoretical issue of determining which goods are global public goods and thus within the domain of governments to provide. But such a focus overlooks the importance of the political process by which such goods come to be recognized and accepted as belonging in that domain. The regulation of the Internet, solutions to preserve the ozone layer, the control of transnational crime — all these have a clear political dimension and thus should be subject to open debate, in which societal differences in norms and values can be expressed and taken into account. Economic, cultural, and social integration requires more than efficient technocratic management; the contentious issues it places on the transnational agenda can only be tackled by inclusive and legitimate political processes, which GPP networks can promote. Many of the cases surveyed as background for this report are telling examples.

Effectiveness and efficiency cannot be the only yardsticks in designing new governance mechanisms; legitimacy and inclusion are equally important, not only in terms of a *Weltanschauung*, but also from a strategic and political perspective. As the breakdown of the negotiations toward the Multilateral Agreement on Investment (MAI) made clear, nonstate actors have successfully reorganized themselves to build transnational coalitions, capable of challenging governance mechanisms they perceive as overly secret, undemocratic, or inequitable. And even if — as some claim — their arguments are faulty, only an open and inclusive debate might bring this to light. As the landmines movement and the Jubilee 2000 coalition have convincingly demonstrated, the failure of international organizations to address concerns based on such norms and values and to act as "norm entrepreneurs" (see Chapter 5) may pressure those public institutions to react, rather than encouraging them to act proactively.

STATES, INTERNATIONAL ORGANIZATIONS, AND THE IMPERATIVE OF CHANGE

States and international organizations thus face profound challenges to their continued ability to execute their mandates. They have yet to respond in a comprehensive and systematic fashion to the new, global economic environment that national and cross-border liberalization and deregulation have created, in a way that takes advantage of the benefits that these processes can bring. And all public institutions must learn how to keep up with the increasing pace of technological innovation and assess its implications for the structure and processes of information and knowledge creation, processing, and implementation as these relate to their own public-policy-making, both nationally and globally.

If the operational and participatory gaps described above are not at some point effectively addressed, the risk of a popular backlash against deeper social and economic integration becomes ever higher. In fact, grass-roots concerns about economic liberalization have already contributed to a massive slowdown in negotiations in this area over the last 10 years, especially with regard to international trade. For example, the Seattle Round of trade liberalization, launched in late 1999 despite widespread popular opposition, shows little prospect of major progress.

Conventional forms of international governance have so far been unable to fill these gaps. Their default has contributed to a growing legitimacy crisis for multilateralism in general, which in turn has fueled the backlash against globalization. For the multilateral institutions, responding in timely fashion to the challenges outlined above will be critical, not only for meeting their mission, but also for ensuring their continued legitimacy. An inadequate response may well jeopardize deeper integration, as governments, in particular, will have little choice but to fall back on territorial solutions to their governance challenges.

Fortunately, some of the same developments that pose such a daunting challenge to traditional governance mechanisms also offer the potential to help bridge both the operational and the participatory gaps. For example, the technological developments that make rapid information flows possible enable the kind of decentralized, non-hierarchical network structure needed to respond quickly and flexibly to a rapidly changing environment. With a mobilized global citizenry, monitoring can take place in a less centralized, more participatory manner, and increasing political liberalization can allow the monitors to become active on a transnational level. There is no guarantee, however, that governance mechanisms will emerge naturally just because the need and the raw materials are there. And the governance mechanisms that do emerge may fail to address critical issues of leadership, inclusion, and funding. Mindful of the opportunities — and the risks — of changes in governance structures and processes, the next two chapters focus on GPP networks as institutional innovations that can contribute to closing both the operational and the participatory gaps in governance.

Chapter 3

WHAT DO NETWORKS DO?

We begin this chapter with a short primer on the most basic attributes of GPP networks (a detailed theoretical analysis would go far beyond the scope of this report; see the bibliography for additional references). We then turn to a discussion, drawing on our case studies, of what we see as the six most important functions of GPP networks and how individual networks have or have not succeeded in executing those functions. It goes without saying that our classification of network activities into these six functions cannot do full justice to the full range of activities reported in the case studies, but it is useful in clarifying the most important issues.

The six functions of GPP networks are as follows:

+ They contribute to establishing a global policy agenda, and then they offer mechanisms for developing a truly global public discourse in which to debate that agenda;

+ They facilitate processes for negotiating and setting global standards;

+ They help develop and disseminate knowledge that is crucial to addressing transnational challenges;

+ They help create and deepen markets;

+ They provide innovative mechanisms for implementing global agreements; and

+ They address the participatory gap by creating inclusive processes that build trust and social capital in the global public space by furthering transnational and transsectoral discourse and interaction.

These functions are not mutually exclusive, to be sure. Many of the case studies reveal networks performing a number of these functions simultaneously.

A PRIMER ON NETWORKS

GPP networks include actors from different sectors. Ideally, they bring together the public sector (states and international public organizations), civil society (NGOs and the like), and the for-profit private sector (corporations, other businesses, and their associations). Indeed, a growing number of transnational challenges require this form of trisectoral collaboration. GPP networks emerged in the shadow of traditional multilateralism. As our cases show, many of them started out as innovative organizational and social experiments, responding to an ever more complex global policy environment, taking advantage of new opportunities for cooperation, and relying to differing degrees on the new medium provided by advances in information and communication technologies (ICTs). Most important, GPP networks developed as a means to bring together far-flung institutions and people who often remain separate and are sometimes opposed to each other but who realize that they depend on each other to reach their differing goals and agree to collaborate in a loose, self-governing structure.

It is important to understand that GPP networks are not just another attempt at organization-building. They are dynamic in both process and structure. They can perhaps best be understood in terms of a four-stage policy cycle:

1. *Agenda-setting* involves raising awareness and pushing issues onto the global agenda;

2. *Negotiation* involves the application of decision-making processes;

3. *Implementation* entails translating the results of negotiations into action and developing or improving a willingness or capacity on the part of stakeholders to comply; and

4. *Policy reformulation and institutional learning* reflect the extent to which built-in mechanisms facilitate learning and change in the network.

This report has refrained from developing a clear-cut typology of GPP networks. Their huge variety of form and development suggests that, to date, they have been situational and opportunistic in nature. This may indicate that a process of evolutionary selection is under way, at the end of which a few particularly successful forms of GPP network will prevail. However, it is too early to predict the course and outcome of this development.

It is important to note that participation of actors from the various sectors in GPP networks usually varies along the policy cycle, as our cases will show. For example, the participation of all major actors (governments, international organizations, the business sector, and civil society) may be indispensable at certain stages of the policy cycle, such as negotiation and implementation, depending on the potential for conflict involved. On the other hand, from a purely analytical perspective at least, the initial setting of agendas would not necessarily require multisector participation, and the empirical picture confirms this.

As indicated above, GPP networks are institutional innovations. But they build on ideas that have been well developed in other fields, such as Elinor Ostrom's idea of "co-production" in smaller local communities, and through research on networks at the national and, in Europe, regional levels. Complementarity of resources is the key to the success of networks. Networks do not merely aggregate resources, but are structured to take advantage of the fact that each participating sector brings different resources to the fore. A typical network (if there is such a thing) combines the voluntary energy and legitimacy of the civil-society sector with the financial muscle and interest of businesses and the enforcement and rule-making power and coordination and capacity-building skills of states and international organizations.

Networks create bridges that enable these various participants to exploit the synergies between these resources. They allow for the pooling of know-how and the exchange of experience. Collaboration in networks creates regularity and predictability in the participants' relationships, generating a feasible institutional framework for fruitful cooperation. Spanning socioeconomic, political, and cultural gaps, networks manage relationships that might otherwise degenerate into counterproductive confrontation, something we have seen too often in recent years with the growing presence of both business and civil society in the global policy arena.

GPP networks not only combine existing knowledge from different sources and backgrounds but also create new knowledge, as consensus emerges over often-contentious issues. This requires knowledge management of a sort that lies beyond the traditional meaning of the term. Relying on differences in knowledge and in opportunities for knowledge-gathering among stakeholders, GPP networks apply an open sourcing model already applied in the private sector and manage knowledge from the bottom up. This model of managing knowledge is far from perfect, but it is a considerable improvement, given that it involves all stakeholders.

An added feature of this form of knowledge management is that it ensures constant learning — from both successes and failures. GPP networks are, in one important dimension, learning organizations, built on the diversity of their participants. Learning in the context of diversity takes advantage of what has been called the "strength of weak ties," making use of the knowledge and experience of participants from different social, cultural, and political backgrounds. But the ability of networks to innovate and learn depends heavily on the talent of network managers to keep these ties loose, but still close enough to be manageable — as one observer put it, networks are exercises in structured informality.

GPP networks both respond to and take advantage of technological developments, as well as ongoing processes of international integration, both political and economic, that challenge traditional mechanisms of governance. Technological advances facilitate the rapid flow of information that makes the decentralized, flexible network structure possible. Political liberalization facilitates the transnational activity of nonstate participants. Nevertheless, collaboration in networks for global public-policy-making also requires adjustment on the part of both the network participants and the existing institutions in charge of public policy, that is, states and international organizations. This raises a number of critical issues with regard to institutional management, learning, and change, which are discussed in more detail in Chapter 4; and specifically with regard to the United Nations, in Chapter 5. After all, there should be no doubt that global public-policy-making through collaborative networks is likely to challenge deeply entrenched political, economic, and bureaucratic interests. Policymakers and bureaucrats will surely try to patch up their organizations with new structures or transpose them to new functions, for as long as possible, but a more genuine overhaul of their governance structures and activities may be needed in the long run.

As we have noted, no systematic research on GPP networks has yet been undertaken. Many of the initiatives surveyed below are fairly young, and the enormous variety of networks we observe in the field suggests that no consistent pattern of network-building under specific circumstances and conditions has yet emerged. This situational and opportunistic character of networks in their present form poses limits to how much a report such as this one can actually deliver in terms of rigorous analysis, conclusions, and recommendations. As time goes by, however, more systematic lessons will surely be drawn. The following sections highlight the lessons learned thus far with respect to the six core functions that networks currently fulfill.

PLACING ISSUES ON THE GLOBAL AGENDA

To some degree, all GPP networks seek to place public-policy issues on the global agenda. The very fact that networks form around particular issues suggests a common view among the participants that these issues deserve further attention at the global level.

There is one set of networks, however, whose principal objective is to pressure states and international organizations to address specific policy issues. These networks, which Margaret Keck and Kathryn Sikkink have labeled "transnational advocacy networks," have been the subject of a growing literature in the field of international politics. We can gain a deeper understanding of their origin and the role they play in global governance by putting this type of network into the broader perspective of GPP networks. Advocacy networks generally form between civil-society groups and individual states to lobby intergovernmental organizations, other states, and the business sector to adopt certain measures. These networks use a variety of methods to bring important issues to the forefront of the global policy-making agenda. Several basic lessons can be drawn from their experiences.

STRATEGIC USE OF MEDIA AND INFLUENTIAL INDIVIDUALS

The first lesson is that the strategic use of the media and the involvement of influential individuals have been critical to the success of advocacy networks' efforts. In the case of the ICBL, a coalition of NGOs and governments of several medium-sized nations forced the landmines issue onto the global agenda. Their efforts led, in 1997, to the signing of the Ottawa Convention. The negotiation of an international treaty can often take 10–15 years, yet pressure from the landmines advocacy network forced governments to act more quickly on this issue. Campaign organizers made effective use of the media, circulating vivid images of the devastation caused by landmines, to raise awareness of the problem and arouse popular sentiment. The involvement of internationally recognized figures, most notably Diana, Princess of Wales, drew further attention and support, contributing to the ultimate success of the campaign.

Modeling itself after the landmines effort, the International Coalition to Stop the Use of Child Soldiers has worked through regional conferences and a core group of governments to raise the issue of children in the military on the list of global priorities. As in the landmines case, active engagement with the media has been important, as has the involvement of influential individuals. Key among these has been Graca Machel, whose 1996 report on the impact of armed conflict on children first raised widespread concern. The Coalition is now pushing for the adoption of an optional protocol to the United Nations Convention on the Rights of the Child, and as Stuart Maslen writes in his case study, "the search goes on for a famous personality that could champion the cause of children used and abused as soldiers."

The international debt-relief movement, led by Jubilee 2000, has similarly demonstrated media savvy in its advocacy efforts, as Elizabeth Donnelly demonstrates in her case study. Working through public figures as diverse as Pope John Paul II and the rock star Bono, the network has attracted widespread attention and support while also generating some controversy.

Another network, Transparency International (TI), adopted a focused approach to the problem of bureaucratic corruption, which it articulated through both a normative framework and an argument based on economic efficiency. TI first succeeded in raising awareness of the complexity of the problem and in pushing the issue onto the agenda of international organizations, states, and affected industries. Although corruption has always been recognized as a problem, the relevant governance institutions, especially the international organizations, had not made it a high priority in their work. (The international organizations were restricted by their mandate from bringing the matter to the fore, but it is also true that their staffs were less than eager to push the issue.) TI therefore saw its task more as one of decrying the lack of open acknowledgment of the problem than as one of addressing a real lack of awareness.

This, of course, had consequences for the strategy that TI chose to make its case. As Fredrik Galtung remarks in his case study, a "single, blunt, blanketing awareness campaign" would not have yielded the desired response. Rather, TI would have to somehow crack the taboo around corruption, without alienating the very people on whom it would rely to make inroads into the problem. To win credibility and to position itself as a capable and powerful partner in cooperative anticorruption efforts, TI chose a two-track strategy. First, it raised awareness among the general public and used the media's interest in stories about corruption to push the issue onto the agenda of international organizations, states, and businesses (the group's annual Corruption Perceptions Index is a good example). Second, TI in many instances served as a policy consultant (for example to the World Bank), providing detailed and high-quality intelligence on issues related to corruption and how to tackle them. Although relying on the media, TI chose a less uncompromising advocacy approach in exchange for a mixture of keeping the issue of corruption on the agenda while trying to work with involved actors to find ways to address it. Having succeeded with its agenda-setting strategy, TI has since moved on to the perhaps more difficult challenge of forging, through its national chapters, what Peter Eigen calls "natural coalitions of change," involving a broad range of actors in the fight against corruption.

HELP FROM ADVOCACY NETWORKS

A second lesson that can be discerned is that advocacy networks can increase the prominence of issues that are already on the global agenda by articulating clear and focused goals, often justifying them on incontrovertible moral grounds. In two of the cases discussed above, networks focused their attention on narrow issues within a broader policy domain: landmines are a form of conventional weapon, and opposition to the use of child soldiers lies within a broader concern for children's rights. In each case, the failure of an earlier intergovernmental convention to adequately address the problem led advocates to push for a network approach, carving out of the broader problem a single issue with a simple and straight-forward moral imperative. Had either group tried to address the issue area on a broader front, their efforts might have been blunted by controversy or a mismatch between their resources and the sheer scope of the problem. Instead, their choice of a specific focus attracted considerable support. The emphasis on normative arguments against the use of landmines and child soldiers also strengthened these networks, in part by depicting opponents' positions as morally indefensible. In similar fashion, the Rugmark Initiative (discussed in Chapter 4) sought to draw attention to the problem of child labour in the carpet industry as a microcosm of a broader social-standards and human-rights agenda.

In a similar manner, the Network on the Development of Guiding Principles for Displacement raised support for its program by using language and norms that had already been approved by states earlier in the process. As Simon Bagshaw writes in his case study, the "greater the number of co-sponsors and the broader the geo-graphical representation, the politically less feasible it becomes for recalcitrant states to obstruct the process."

SUPPORT FROM UNCONVENTIONAL PARTNERS

A third lesson is that advocacy networks can often frame issues in such a way as to attract support from unconventional partners. The Jubilee 2000 campaign for debt relief provides an interesting example. Early on in the campaign, organizers considered changing the campaign's name to Debt Relief 2000. Advertising consultants had cautioned that many people would be unaware that the original, biblical meaning of *jubilee* referred to a custom of periodic, wholesale debt forgiveness. But the network leaders decided to stick to the original name. And as it turned out, the jubilee concept became particularly important in attracting support from churches and religious people. By framing the issue in terms of religious norms, the network formed an improbable coalition between the left-leaning supporters already likely to be drawn to the cause and elements of the Christian right. In another case, Greenpeace framed discussions about global climate change as a hard-headed matter of risk management, rather than only as a soft-hearted matter of protecting fragile ecospheres. With this approach, it succeeded in attracting the banking and insurance industry to participate in the negotiations, as discussed below. How global networks frame public-policy issues can thus be an important element of best-practice networking.

Successful advocacy networks thus make strategic use of the media and influential individuals, articulate clear goals (often through a normative lens), and frame issues so as to have maximum impact. They create a transnational public discourse around policy issues that require a global approach. In many cases, networks that perform functions other than advocacy start in a similar fashion, that is, by placing issues prominently on the global agenda, before moving onto the other phases of the policy cycle. In cases such as the networks on landmines and the use of child soldiers, organizers plan to work on implementing international conventions on their issues once they have successfully lobbied for their adoption. The transnational linkages formed during the advocacy process will likely assist such networks as they move toward implementing policy solutions. More and more advocacy networks have realized that, to move beyond mere advocacy, they must reach out to, and collaborate with, sectors other than their own — in particular the business community.

NEGOTIATING AND SETTING STANDARDS AND REGULATIONS

Setting transnational rules and standards is becoming ever more important as political and economic liberalization and technological change create transnational social and economic spheres of activity whose governance demands a global framework. More and more national and international bureaucracies have realized that negotiating and setting standards to address transnational problems differ from agenda-setting in their need to involve all the stakeholders, both because these stakeholders provide timely and complex knowledge and because their involvement gives legitimacy to the process. A growing number of standards and regulatory issues — from financial regulation to environmental protection, from social standards to public health — have become matters of transnational concern, and managing conflicting knowledge and achieving consensus on particular issues have become core functions of GPP networks. Such networks, as our cases show, are more likely to arise out of a crisis or stalemate, when those in conflict realize that no single group can resolve the issue by itself.

Two of our cases illustrate innovative approaches to negotiating and setting global norms and standards that contributed to closing both the operational and the participatory gaps described in Chapter 2. First, the case of the WCD shows how a truly global trisectoral network was key to overcoming stalemate in the highly controversial and complex policy arena of large-dam construction. Second, the case of the Apparel Industry Partnership (AIP) demonstrates how a network addressing a lack of adequate transnational labour standards was launched at the national level. A third case, that of ISO 14000, may not be an example of best-practice trisectoral standards-setting, but it provides valuable insight into this important function of networks. In a fourth case, the Network on the Development of Guiding Principles for Displacement, network participants focused on a variety of existing norms that had already been approved by many governments in a different human-rights context to rally widespread support for their initiative to negotiate standards for the treatment of internally displaced people. All four cases demonstrate the broad spectrum of issues for which standards-setting is critical, and they have in common the building of consensual knowledge, for which an inclusive approach and the casting of a broad knowledge net are key.

THE WORLD COMMISSION ON DAMS

The case of the WCD demonstrates how an almost archetypical trisectoral network operating at the global level can contribute to building consensual knowledge and overcoming stalemate in a policy arena riven with conflict. The mandate of the WCD is to "undertake a global review of the development effectiveness of large dams and to develop internationally acceptable criteria and guidelines for future decision-making on dams" (Box 5). The network was designed to respond to the operational and participatory governance challenge of generating the institutional arrangements and decision-making processes needed so that dam-building can contribute to achieving sustainable development.

As Sanjeev Khagram demonstrates in his case study of the WCD, the growing complexity and politicization of large-dam construction and its social, economic, and environmental implications made this one of the most conflict-ridden issues in the development debate. In the late 1980s and early 1990s, a breakdown of dialogue among NGOs, builders, and international organizations such as the World Bank, which had financed many large dam projects worldwide, led to a stalemate. This stalemate imposed considerable costs on all stakeholders: builders saw their income from dam construction decline dramatically; NGOs had to spend considerable resources to sustain public campaigns against large dams; and the World Bank, facing fierce public pressure, could no longer support any loans in this area. Bringing representatives from all relevant groups and sectors together in an independent trisectoral network to break the stalemate and to start to form a consensus on standards for large-dam construction was imperative. Their experience might hold important lessons for similar cases, such as the regulation of genetically modified organisms.

The example of the WCD shows that establishing a basic measure of trust among actors in a conflict-ridden environment is time-consuming and costly, but launching a sustainable mechanism for consensus-building and standards-setting requires no less. In the

Box 5

The World Commission on Dams

~ The WCD was initiated jointly by opponents and advocates of large dams to
   review the effectiveness of dam construction for development and to explore
   alternatives for managing water resources;

~ It aims to develop international standards that will assist future decision-making
   about the planning, design, monitoring, and operation of dams;

~ It has a 2-year mandate that expires in June 2000;

~ Its charter emphasizes the goal of establishing an independent, transparent,
   knowledge-driven, and inclusive system that takes into account the interests
   of all stakeholders;

~ The organization's mandate and the choice of its commissioners were subject to
   open deliberation among representatives of all sectors;

~ The WCD provides for monitoring of its various initiatives through case studies, a
   review process, and various consultations at the regional level;

~ It has initiated 10 case studies, designed to collect data relevant to their country
   settings in Brazil, China, India, Norway, Pakistan, Thailand, Turkey, the United
   States, Zambia, and Zimbabwe;

~ It has commissioned 17 thematic reviews, to have been completed in November
   1999, that address social, environmental, economic, and institutional issues
   concerning water-resource management;

~ It will review a total of 150 dams worldwide through a cross-check survey that
   will ensure the accuracy of the case studies' conclusions;

~ It will undertake regional consultations in Africa, East Asia, Latin America, the
   Middle East, and South Asia to increase stakeholder input and information
   exchange;

~ It established the WCD Forum, a 55-member committee that acts as a reference
   group and allows increased consultations among all sectors of society;

~ It accepts only financial contributions that are not tied to any single project
   but are spread across all sectors (to maintain the commission's independence
   and credibility); and

~ It has a total projected budget of about $8.5 million for the duration of the
   initiative.

For more about the WCD, see **www.dams.org** on the Internet.

spring of 1997, the World Conservation Union (International Union for the Conservation of Nature and Natural Resources [IUCN]) and a small group of World Bank staff began an experimental dialogue that brought together both champions and critics of large dams. It took more than a year before the WCD was born, in the summer of 1998. Virtually every decision made in that interim was hotly contested, from the selection of a chairperson, to the number and composition of commission members, to the appropriate roles of the Bank, the IUCN, and other participating groups. However, the fact that these decisions were negotiated in an inclusive and participatory way, with no major interest excluded from the table, was critical to the ultimate establishment of the WCD.

One of the biggest challenges for the WCD was to bring the for-profit private sector on board. Operating in a highly competitive environment, private engineering and construction companies were much less accustomed than the other participants to engaging in collective action, beyond the usual lobbying. However, many followed the lead of Göran Lindahl, president of the multinational engineering firm ABB, who understood early on that a trisectoral effort could lead to greater stability and predictability in the industry's business environment. Unfortunately, established professional associations, such as the International Commission on Large Dams, regarded the WCD as a rival, and only slowly was a measure of trust built up that allowed for meaningful cooperation and negotiation. And, in many cases, getting government approval for local reviews of large dam projects — an integral part of the WCD's work program — has been difficult, as some governments at first perceived the WCD as a biased intruder.

The case of the WCD also shows that truly trisectoral sourcing of knowledge is key for building consensual knowledge and closing the operational and participatory governance gaps. Inclusiveness, openness, and transparency are the key principles of the WCD. Its structure, process, and funding are all trisectoral (see Box 5). Through a number of local reviews of existing dams, the WCD involved both supporters and opponents of dam projects in the gathering of knowledge. This body of knowledge on the complex social, economic, and ecological implications of dam-building is

helping to close both the operational and the participatory gaps.
If the WCD's work is successful, there will be a better understanding
of the impact of large dams, and the trisectoral sourcing of this
knowledge will have created a more participatory process around the
issue. The local reviews of existing dam projects also involve local
communities and will enable them to better understand the impact
of large dams.

The time-boundedness of the commission's work (the WCD will
dissolve in 2000, after 2 years in operation) is an important
precondition for the success of the WCD to date. The participants
made a commitment that the work program of the WCD would be
completed within the specified period, after which the commission
will cease to exist. Setting a time limit on the commission's activities
ensures that the results will be useful to various stakeholders
because of their timeliness, and it guarantees that the WCD will
not degenerate into just another talk shop unable to admit its
growing irrelevance.

The strictly trisectoral nature of the WCD has thus been critical for
its success to date. In part, this is also because sharing funding
responsibilities across all sectors has ensured its continued credibility (see Chapter 4). A valuable lesson of this case is that the more
conflict-ridden an issue area is, the more important the trisectoral
nature of the endeavour becomes.

THE APPAREL INDUSTRY PARTNERSHIP

Whereas the WCD is a truly global network, the AIP is an example of
a network that addresses a similarly controversial transnational issue
starting at the domestic level. The AIP brought together a group of
US-based multinational companies, NGOs, and organized labour,
through the initiative of the US government, to negotiate a voluntary
code of conduct for multinational companies in the clothing
industry (Box 6). This unilateral US initiative responded to an
intergovernmental failure to address the growing complexity and
geographic scope of labour-rights issues more generally. Although
labour standards, especially the banning of child labour and sweatshops, have been on the agenda of international organizations for a
long time, national and international regulatory efforts have been

largely unsuccessful. The International Labour Organization (ILO) and other bodies have promoted these issues but have fallen short of eliminating these practices. It was this failure of international code-building efforts to construct meaningful instruments for enforcement that opened the door to nonstate initiatives to address labour standards.

Responding to the failure of intergovernmental regulatory approaches and the need to bring business and civil society on board in a constructive fashion, the US Department of Labor suggested a US-based approach toward standards-setting, relying on voluntary, rather than top-down, hierarchical, regulation. At the time, this national approach also made sense because the huge number of actors worldwide affected by labour standards made coordination

---

Box 6
The Apparel Industry Partnership

~ The AIP was initiated in August 1996, after US President Bill Clinton brought leaders of the apparel and footwear industry, labour unions, consumer groups, and human-rights NGOs together to work to ensure that products are manufactured under decent and humane working conditions and to communicate that information to consumers;

~ It adopted, in April 1997, a code of conduct defining decent and humane working conditions and adopted principles for monitoring the code;

~ It established the Fair Labor Association, a not-for-profit organization, to develop an independent external monitoring system and appropriate consumer education mechanisms;

~ It has as its lead governmental actor the US Department of Labor, which has shown renewed vigour in promoting labour standards at home and abroad;

~ It includes as participants in the network 10 private companies and 1 business association;

~ It includes as participants 4 nonprofit human-rights and labour NGOs, although 1 religious NGO and 2 union representatives withdrew in November 1998; and

~ It has also been influenced by many actors outside the network, including student activist groups such as United Students Against Sweatshops, the socially responsible investor community, and religious groups.

For more about the AIP, see the documents at **www.laborrights.org/aip/index.html**, made available on the Internet through the International Labor Rights Fund.

extremely difficult. It was clear that all US stakeholders needed to cooperate in order to abolish the offensive practices. It was also recognized that all efforts to eliminate sweatshops had to focus on continuously improving working conditions abroad. Of course, the initiative would have a cross-border impact, as, under the agreement, the overseas suppliers of US-based apparel firms are also supposed to open their production sites for monitoring. An international expansion of the network is also on the agenda, which will primarily involve drawing into the process multinationals not based in the United States.

The AIP case shows how hard it is to close the governance gap by developing labour standards for transnationally networked companies, even when starting out with a limited, national approach involving a small number of players. Not surprisingly, given that multinationals, organized labour, and NGOs were all at the table, the negotiations remained highly contentious throughout. Yet, US apparel companies had two major incentives to join the AIP. First, they wanted to avoid further public embarrassment, as well as economic losses arising from such debacles as the discovery of apparel sweatshops in El Monte, California. Second, they recognized that, in many cases, improving the conditions of labour would actually increase productivity and product quality. For the NGOs, the prospect of being able to arm-twist some apparel companies into recognizing their responsibilities to their workers and into coming to the negotiating table to join efforts to fight sweatshops was important in itself. In addition, the participation of some apparel companies in AIP drove a wedge between them and other companies that had not recognized their responsibilities to workers and consumers. This was something the NGOs could use as leverage, both to hold those firms in the AIP accountable to higher standards of behaviour and to pressure those outside the AIP to follow the example of the industry leaders. (For more on the exploitation of intrasectoral differences in networks, see Chapter 4.)

AIP members found out early in their deliberations that achieving consensus on labour standards is extremely time-consuming and difficult. However, they also acknowledged that collaboration was

key to the integrity and credibility of the resulting code and principles of monitoring and that it allowed some trust to be developed
between NGOs and companies. The bargaining power of the various
parties was more or less equal: the industry could rely on its
superior financial resources, and the NGOs could rely on their
"shaming" strategies, whereby they arranged for media exposure
of scandalous corporate practices. This can best be seen, as David
Bobrowsky argues in his case study, in the compromises worked out
over what kind of monitoring the AIP would agree to and who would
pay for it. Whereas the NGOs were keenly interested in establishing
effective monitoring, the companies sought to avoid agreeing to
independent external monitors. Despite the company representatives' assurances that internal monitoring would be sufficient,
the NGOs stuck firmly to the principle of external monitoring, and
ultimately they prevailed. After long and difficult negotiations that
several times came close to breaking down, all parties agreed on a
common set of standards and an external monitoring process. The
participants agreed to set up the Fair Labor Association (FLA), an
independent NGO tasked with handling the accreditation of independent monitors, certifying compliance with the AIP's code of
conduct, and serving as a clearinghouse for information exchange
and further negotiations.

Their successes to date notwithstanding, the challenges for the AIP
and the FLA remain formidable. All participants have had to make
compromises, which have led to complications within their own
sectors. Indeed, organized labour eventually pulled out of the
process, feeling that voluntary codes of conduct would not satisfy
their demands. Within the NGO community, meanwhile, there are
conflicts between radicals and moderates. The case of the AIP also
shows that public backing that depends on the electoral cycle can
severely hurt a network. Labour standards proved not to be an
attractive campaign issue in upcoming elections, and the US government stopped pushing the issue. After initially using the partnership
to generate good press, the government no longer gives the network
the same level of public recognition. Furthermore, the number of
participating companies is growing very slowly, partly because of the
lessening of public governmental pressure and partly because of
increasing competition in labels and codes of conduct from other
companies and networks.

The case of the AIP shows that the move from the negotiation phase of the policy cycle to actual implementation is a critical one that carries substantial risks. Provided the implementation phase takes off, the next critical issue for the AIP will be to attract new members, especially from other countries, into the network. Indeed, although the national approach may have simplified the task of launching negotiations and the effective implementation of core labour standards (such as the ban on child labour), the network can only truly claim success once the codes have spread worldwide.

ISO 14000

Standards-setting through the ISO 14000 process is another example of a network-driven response to the growing complexity and geographic scope of global environmental issues. The ISO 14000 set of environmental management standards diverges from typical standards negotiated previously under the umbrella of the International Standardization Organization (ISO) in that it addresses issues that are recognized as having complex social and political implications.

In principle, the ISO's move to tackle new process standards is welcome. The organization has comparative advantage in standards-setting because of its long-standing experience and extensive knowledge in that field. The wealth of knowledge available to it and the broad participation of industry, often lacking in other standards-setting approaches, qualify the ISO as a platform for such negotiations. However, the ISO 14000 process also exemplifies a lack of built-in organizational learning mechanisms, given that the ISO has thus far failed to sufficiently transform itself to serve as an appropriate venue for process standards. To gain broad acceptance of standards, procedures of consultation and rule-setting have to be transparent, inclusive, and open. ISO standards-setting is usually long, complicated, and highly decentralized, as the detailed negotiations are carried out through technical committees, subcommittees, and working groups. These have typically been industry dominated, given that businesses usually set the agenda by proposing new product standards in the first place.

To many NGOs and developing countries, the standards-setting procedures applied under ISO 14000 appeared opaque and expensive, as Virginia Haufler points out in her case study. Many developing countries lack the capacity, in terms of both knowledge and financial resources, to attend the numerous meetings. Although some ISO delegations have sought to include NGOs in their deliberations, for many NGOs (especially smaller ones) the unfamiliarity with ISO processes and the lack of financial means have been barriers to effective participation. Many NGOs also regard ISO procedures with suspicion, viewing the process as dominated by business.

If the ISO is ever to become a lead forum in the setting of environmental management standards, it will have to adapt its internal procedures considerably to make the process more transparent. It will also have to engage in capacity-building to allow the meaningful participation of developing countries and NGOs. One way to begin thinking about this challenge is to look at the example of the Global Environment Facility (GEF), which managed to transform itself from a purely intergovernmental organization into a more open forum that places a premium on capacity-building. (See "Implementing ideas and decisions," later in this chapter, and "Tackling the dual challenge of inclusion," in Chapter 4.) To be sure, the ISO has improved a lot in the process of hosting the negotiations for the ISO 14000 set of standards. The ISO Secretariat and others are launching more and more initiatives to increase capacity in developing countries, though it is too early to determine how effective these are. NGOs were able to move up the learning curve and are in some cases more effective partners today than they were a few years ago.

The case of environmental standards illustrates the confusion in the current regime of global standards-setting. There have been countless attempts — local, national, regional, and global — to regulate standards in various fields, such as the environment, labour, or human rights more broadly. Some, such as the AIP, have also been sector specific. When a labeling strategy aimed at influencing consumer behaviour accompanies voluntary standards and codes of conduct, the chaos resulting from the proliferation of diverse labels can cause a loss of confidence in the standards and regulations and thus a loss in their effectiveness. Although it is questionable whether a centralized global approach is needed in all cases, the time has come to consolidate these processes by sharing information and disseminating best practices and to focus activities on a few forums rather than many. One possible role of the United Nations and its specialized agencies could be to coordinate these efforts (see Chapter 5).

The Network on the Development of Guiding Principles for Displacement

At times, GPP networks must devise strategies to achieve their goals in the face of potential opposition from governments. In contrast to cases such as the ICBL and the International Coalition to Stop the Use of Child Soldiers, actors in the global Network on the Development of Guiding Principles for Displacement specifically chose not to lobby for a new international legal instrument. They recognized that the state-dominated process of ratifying a treaty or declaration would be too difficult, especially given the questions of sovereignty involved in the problem of people being displaced within their own countries. Instead, the network adopted the strategy of compiling existing international legal norms into a set of Guiding Principles for Displacement. By using language and norms that had already been ratified by governments and a mandate approved by the General Assembly of the United Nations, network managers sought to win support from a wide range of member states.

Through these strategies, the network was able to form a broad coalition of state support. As Simon Bagshaw shows, in the case of Mexico, the government continued to object because it saw this process as a form of standards-setting through the back door. Nevertheless, the network managed to get other states on board and to push the Guiding Principles through an approval process less complicated than a treaty ratification or declaration would have been. According to Bagshaw,

> The key point to arise from the development of the Guiding Principles within a GPP framework is that the elaboration of an international treaty, giving rise to binding obligations for those states which sign and ratify it, is not necessarily a prerequisite for providing an effective normative framework.

As these four cases have shown, where issues are contentious, a participatory and inclusive approach, using open sourcing to pool knowledge, is imperative for producing effective and politically sustainable results. In addition, successful standards-setting does not end with agreement on a norm. Rather, it must proceed to implementation and compliance, which in turn require ownership of the process by those with a stake in the outcome. The case of the AIP has clearly shown that implementation may bring a new stage of conflict, with which the network must then come to terms.

DEVELOPING AND DISSEMINATING KNOWLEDGE

Developing and sharing knowledge are key to all networks, but some networks take specific advantage of the opportunities provided by technological change to enable people and institutions facing similar problems to develop, share, and disseminate knowledge on how best to address the challenges they face. Technology and the information revolution allow best practices and solutions to be shared with increasing ease and at ever-lower cost. CGIAR is an example of a network that exploits economies of scale in developing and sharing scientific knowledge on how best to address the food crisis in the developing world (Box 7). The Roll Back Malaria (RBM) initiative is a network dedicated to better coordination of public and private efforts in the fight against malaria (Box 8).

THE CONSULTATIVE GROUP ON INTERNATIONAL AGRICULTURAL RESEARCH

One of the oldest public-policy networks, CGIAR relies on economies of scale to create and disseminate knowledge about high-yielding crop varieties, food-production systems, and food policies to help developing countries fight poverty and food insecurity. CGIAR is an alliance of 58 donors brought together by its cosponsors: the Food and Agricultural Organization of the United Nations (FAO), the United Nations Development Programme (UNDP), the United Nations Environment Programme (UNEP), and the World Bank. It supports 16 international agricultural research centres. CGIAR's experience shows the importance of having a simple yet important goal, a clear focus and methodology for approaching that goal, and a flexible organizational structure for realizing it. Its informal

Box 7

The Consultative Group on International Agricultural Research

~ CGIAR was established in 1971, as an informal network of international organizations, bilateral donor agencies, and private foundations, to support international agricultural research centres for developing countries;

~ It was stimulated by the success of the International Rice Research Institute in the Philippines and the International Center for the Improvement of Maize and Wheat in Mexico in making the green revolution possible through high-yielding varieties of rice and wheat;

~ It has a mission to contribute to food security and poverty eradication in developing countries through research, partnership, capacity-building, and policy support and to promote sustainable agricultural development based on the environmentally sound management of natural resources;

~ Currently, it has 58 donor members, including 22 developing or transitional economies, supporting 16 research centres with an operating budget of $350 million (the 5 top donors are the European Union, Japan, Switzerland, the United States, and the World Bank);

~ Through its research centres, it conducts research on food commodities, sustainable food-production systems, and food policy, and it works to build the capacity of national agricultural research systems;

~ It operates on a partnership basis with research institutions in developing and industrialized countries;

~ It works to ensure that benefits from its research are international public goods freely available for use in the public and private sectors;

~ Through research on commodities, production systems, and policy, it has had an important impact on food production and incomes in many Southern countries and, to a lesser extent, in the North (recently, it has devoted increased resources to impact assessment);

~ It pioneered the use of information technology for system management and stays abreast of best practices for collecting and disseminating information and stimulating interaction;

~ It helps to ensure biodiversity through the maintenance of collections at several centres that together make up the largest store of plant germplasm relevant to tropical and subtropical agriculture (these collections are held under the auspices of the FAO, with a policy of unrestricted availability [subject in recent years to the constraints of various international agreements]); and

~ In the 1990s, it established new structures to enhance the participation and influence of stakeholders, including national research systems in the South, civil society, and private business.

Find out more about CGIAR at **www.cgiar.org** on the Internet.

Box 8
The Roll Back Malaria initiative

~ The RBM was launched jointly by the World Health Organization (WHO), the World Bank, the United Nations Children's Fund (UNICEF), and the UNDP in November 1998;

~ It involves international organizations, bilateral development agencies, businesses, NGOs, and the media;

~ It seeks to reduce mortality resulting from malaria by 50% by 2010 and by 75% by 2015;

~ It is designed to improve the general health system in countries where malaria is endemic by strengthening the various sectors of the health-care community, including the public health system, civil society, and private providers;

~ It has identified six strategic areas as key for malaria control and prevention: early detection, rapid treatment, preventive measures, improved coordination, a cohesive global movement, and improved research;

~ It has established partnerships with regional stakeholders, representatives of various sectors of society, industry partners, and the research community to ensure the proper use and distribution of resources;

~ It relies on a central team of 8–10 WHO staff members to coordinate its various activities;

~ Although RBM is not a financing instrument, it intends to support countries in their fight against malaria by giving them access to knowledge, technology, and financial resources through global partnerships;

~ It receives funds from WHO, the World Bank, UNICEF, and five bilateral donors: Germany, the Netherlands, Norway, Sweden, and the United Kingdom; and

~ It has a forecast budget of $25 million for 2000.

Find out more about RBM at **www.who.int/rbm/about.html** on the Internet.

structure (the group itself has no independent legal status, and secretariat and technical support are provided through the World Bank and the FAO) has fostered trust and commitment among the donors and centres.

In contrast to the ISO, CGIAR has changed its activities and adjusted its structure over time to take account of fresh challenges. The pace of change has been incremental over most of CGIAR's life, but it has accelerated in recent years. A Genetic Resources Policy Committee was established in 1994 to help deal with conflicting and controversial new international regulations on the ownership and use of plant germplasm. CGIAR currently spends around 9% of its resources on biotechnology research and is studying how its priorities and its structure may be affected by this powerful but controversial new set of instruments. These two fields, germplasm ownership and biotechnology, both involving issues of intellectual property rights, illustrate how a network established to disseminate consensual knowledge can be drawn into more contentious waters. In 1995, CGIAR set up advisory committees to improve two-way communication with NGOs and the private sector. And in 1996, it stimulated the creation of the Global Forum on Agricultural Research (GFAR) in response to criticisms that CGIAR was unnecessarily exclusive — that it had neglected to give full weight to developing-country participation and to reach out to civil society in general. GFAR provides a venue where all stakeholders in the field of agricultural research can make their voices heard and propose initiatives to be considered in CGIAR and elsewhere.

CGIAR's experience also shows that the use and continual upgrading of information technology are critical for a network that deals primarily in research and the dissemination of results. This fact can be illustrated in many dimensions. According to one commentator,

> *In the past, indigenous knowledge about local varieties, farming techniques, and other local technologies tested through the generations rarely made its way to scientists who could incorporate it in their work. Now this knowledge, combined with new and classical scientific knowledge, is available worldwide.*

Maurice Strong, who chaired the most recent system-wide review of CGIAR, described his vision of CGIAR's future role by saying that

> *New scientific developments have the potential to radically reshape the world's agriculture and food systems ... we need to recommit to science and research to ensure that the poor are not excluded, and that biodiversity and the environment are not undermined.*

THE ROLL BACK MALARIA INITIATIVE

The RBM initiative is another network that creates, shares, and disseminates knowledge. It does so primarily through better coordination of previously existing initiatives in malaria control and by bringing both civil society and the business sector into the fight against malaria to a greater extent than before. This emphasis on sharing knowledge across sectors can serve as a model for many other GPP networks and is one the ISO could certainly learn from.

As Arjen van Ballegoyen shows in his case study, RBM's trisectoral approach builds on the lessons learned from a number of unsuccessful initiatives by the World Health Organization (WHO) to fight diseases endemic to developing countries, including malaria. By bringing together the available knowledge from all three sectors, the RBM initiative hopes to increase efficiency and efficacy and avoid duplication of effort in malaria control. The core organizations already had parts of their machinery working on malaria. However, communication between their staffs was extremely poor: people in the various organizations often did not know each other and sometimes did not even know that similar work was being done elsewhere. This was a problem not just at the transnational level, but even at the local level. Thus, one direct benefit derived from the meetings held so far under RBM's aegis is the simple fact that staff members of the various organizations have established contact with each other.

The RBM initiative shows that making full use of the differing comparative advantages of network participants is crucial for networks engaged in coordinating research activities. In the past, reliance on this principle had been limited by the lack of interagency communication, and this had led to agencies taking on tasks in which they had no particular advantage, or it led to tasks simply not being undertaken at all. The reapplication and strengthening of this principle — that is, the switch to sector-wide approaches and the renewed requirement for communication across organizations and sectors — will require a lot of learning and a change in organizational cultures. This will not be easy, and it will take time. If it succeeds, it will be because the process has been fueled from the bottom up, from the operational side, making use of the principle of open sourcing. It is on the operational side of the endeavour that people are meeting and working together creatively to solve problems, building trust that in turn will lead to a tighter knit community of researchers committed to the conquest of malaria.

THE URBAN MANAGEMENT PROGRAMME

The Urban Management Programme (UMP) is yet another effort to coordinate and exchange knowledge, in this case knowledge related to participatory urban governance, alleviation of urban poverty, and urban environmental management (Box 9). As demonstrated in Oluwemimo Oluwasola's case study, the UMP's trisectoral interaction takes place at the local level in the form of multisectoral city consultations. The network ensures the exchange of experiences gained at the local level, building a larger knowledge base from the bottom up. The network thus provides a structure through which cities in developing countries can learn from the development successes (and failures) of other urban areas within their regions and around the world.

Developing and sharing knowledge are prerequisites for the continuous cycle of learning and policy reformulation that underlies the functioning of all networks. All too often, networks are merely reactive, but if they take full advantage of the opportunities that the global information revolution offers, networks that develop, share, and disseminate knowledge can be truly proactive, as they can spread the lessons learned from failures as well as successes.

MAKING AND DEEPENING MARKETS

GPP networks can act as bridges between producers and buyers, borrowers and lenders, to make markets where they are lacking and to deepen markets where they are not fulfilling their potential. Left to their own devices, markets sometimes fail to produce certain goods whose provision would be in the broader public interest. This can be seen at the global as well as the local level. The fight against infectious diseases is one issue area where GPP networks are contributing to the creation of markets by helping to develop and distribute vaccines against diseases such as malaria. The microcredit industry is an area where networks are deepening markets, by extending the market for credit to the poor. By building bridges and expanding markets, GPP networks take advantage of technological change and new possibilities for cooperation.

Box 9
The Urban Management Programme

~ The UMP was initiated in 1986 to develop and apply knowledge in the fields of participatory urban governance, urban poverty alleviation, and urban environmental management;

~ It seeks to strengthen the contribution that cities and towns in developing countries make toward human development, participatory governance, social equity, economic efficiency, and poverty reduction;

~ It has regional offices in Africa, Asia, the Caribbean, Latin America, and the Middle East, which respond to requests for assistance from local authorities, using resources provided by the participating stakeholders;

~ Through its local offices, it allows for substantive input through consultations on urban management issues, support for regional experts, and aid in global strategy formulation;

~ It uses action plans and consultations to provide information about policy guidelines at the city, country, regional, and global levels;

~ In 1999, it initiated City Development Strategies to define urban priorities, using analyses of individual cities, frequent consultations with mayors, and the participation of residents;

~ The UMP is administered at the global level by the United Nations Centre for Human Settlements (UNCHS [Habitat]) in Nairobi;

~ It is organized as a partnership of the UNDP, the UNCHS, the World Bank, and the governments of the Netherlands, Sweden, Switzerland, and the United Kingdom; and

~ It has a budget exceeding $4.5 million for 2000.

Find out more about the UMP at **www.hsd.ait.ac.th/ump/aua.html** on the Internet.

THE MEDICINES FOR MALARIA VENTURE

The new Medicines for Malaria Venture (MMV, now part of RBM) is a good example. The MMV was launched to solve the problem of private-sector underinvestment in vaccine research and production and thus to respond to a steady decrease in private involvement in malaria prevention and control since the 1960s (Box 10). The MMV seeks to create incentives for the development of new drugs and vaccines and thus to spur the development of new medicines that would otherwise never be brought to market.

Box 10
The Medicines for Malaria Venture

~ The MMV has set as its goal to secure the registration (every 5 years, on average) of one new antimalarial drug affordable to the worst-hit populations and capable of countering the growing resistance to existing vaccines (more than 1 million people still die from malaria each year);

~ It offers an effective solution to this health problem through a partnership between the pharmaceutical industry (with its expertise in drug development) and the public sector (with its knowledge of field studies and basic biological research);

~ It effectively acts as a bridge between academic institutions (which perform the basic research) and medical communities (which treat and control malaria);

~ It brought together inaugural partners from all sectors of society, including WHO, the International Federation of Pharmaceutical Manufacturers Associations, the World Bank, the Government of the Netherlands, the UK Department for International Development, the Swiss Agency for Development and Cooperation, the Global Forum for Health Research, the Rockefeller Foundation, and the RBM partnership;

~ It is managed on a day-to-day basis by a management team, operationally independent of the donors, which fosters and coordinates the appropriation of MMV resources;

~ It expects to receive funds from governmental agencies, philanthropic donations, and foundations totaling $15 million a year by 2001 and $30 million a year soon thereafter;

~ If funding efforts are successful, it will make its first product commercially available before 2010; and

~ It is structured as an entrepreneurial, not-for-profit business venture that will funnel royalties from its products into a general fund to offset the need for future donations.

For more about MMV visit **www.malariamedicines.org** on the Internet.

The reasons that deterred major drug companies from getting involved in malaria research were purely economic. Research into malaria vaccines is a complex endeavour, and there is wide agreement that discovery of an effective vaccine will take at least another decade. This long and uncertain time horizon makes malaria vaccine research a very costly undertaking. Businesses contemplating entry have no assurance that they can recover their upfront costs. On the demand side, meanwhile, the purchasing power in the potential market for such a vaccine is small: most of the countries where malaria is endemic are poor. Hence, making a profit seems out of the question; breaking even may be the best anyone can hope for. Under these circumstances, the challenge for the MMV is to intervene in the market to try to change the dismal incentive structure facing potential vaccine producers, in the hope of reviving their interest and mobilizing them for a renewed push toward development and distribution of an effective vaccine.

Clearly, the malaria victims in developing countries are the ones who suffer most from this underinvestment. But overcoming this market failure is also in the interests of developed countries, given that some researchers expect to see the return of malaria to the United States and other developed countries in the coming decade.

With the MMV, a new NGO has been created in which industry and civil society can collaborate to ensure adequate funding for research. Contributors to the MMV include, among others, the Global Forum for Health Research, the Rockefeller Foundation, the SmithKline Beecham and Wellcome Trust, the UK Department for International Development, the International Federation of Pharmaceutical Manufacturers Associations, and the Association of British Pharmaceutical Industries, as well as the World Bank. Research and development are funded primarily by the public sector and private foundations, thus creating a more predictable business environment for the pharmaceutical companies that have made a commitment to provide expertise and resources. However, any vaccine discoveries will be patented, and the owner of those patents will be the MMV. In turn, pharmaceutical companies will be allowed to market the products to low-income populations at affordable prices. A royalty income may go to the MMV on those products that earn significant returns for the organization's commercial partners. These returns will be fed back into the MMV's funds, to diminish the need for future donations. Through the new initiative, the private and public sectors aim to bring together the best of each other's strengths. By creating a market mechanism for the distribution of vaccines, the MMV contributes to RBM's ambitious goal of halving the global malaria burden by 2010. In addition, the MMV initiative highlights the fact that promoting GPP networks in these fields is an investment in a global health infrastructure, not just aid.

NETWORKS FOR MICROLENDING

Trisectoral networks can also support the deepening of existing markets to include those who would otherwise not have access. Microlending networks are a case in point. Microlending — the extension of small loans to poor individuals and small businesses — is regarded as one of the most effective tools yet invented for combating poverty. Microlending networks bring together NGOs, the public sector (donor agencies and international organizations), and commercial banks to support such financing. As Anna Ohanyan describes in her case study, individual microcredit enterprises, which are often trisectoral in composition, are sustained through close linkages among a variety of actors, including states, central banks, commercial banks, local NGOs, and foundations. Although individual microlending initiatives are basically oriented to this one issue, they do more than deliver a financial service. They also generate sociopolitical outcomes, strengthen self-governance capacities at the local level (through the financing of educational programs and, in some cases, the delivery of health care), and empower the poor.

Although a global approach is by no means essential to make microlending work, the presence of economies of scale, the potential to share best practices, and reasons of simple efficiency make it the preferred approach from the perspective of international organizations and other supporters. The Consultative Group to Assist the Poor, a network consisting of microlending practitioners and donor organizations, aims to support institutional development in microfinance and improve the quality of the industry's operations by supporting changes in donors' practices that will further improve the quality of their activities related to microfinance. The group also seeks to expand existing knowledge on how to maximize the outreach of microfinance institutions to the poor and how to upgrade the legal and regulatory framework in which such institutions operate. The commercialization of the industry, necessary to make it sustainable over time, is a medium- to long-term goal. Attracting the private sector into individual microlending networks is also needed to diversify the sources of funding.

The use of technology is central to microlending and its future development. Cost-effective e-mail communication between the industrial-country headquarters of microfinance institutions and their field offices in the developing world is of critical importance. The World Wide Web is increasingly used to manage knowledge and disseminate information on best practices. The *Virtual Library on Microcredit* (www.soc.titech.ac.jp/icm/) contains contact information about practitioners and donors, as well as academic articles and papers about microcredit. Using the World Wide Web to wire together a large number of microcredit groups around the world holds huge promise for advancing and extending the practice — and for making it more attractive to commercial banks. Web-based initiatives such as PlaNet Finance (www.planetfinance.org) can help connect microfinance institutions all over the world, allowing them to share best practices and even to rate different initiatives according to their efficiency and effectiveness in serving the poor. This also involves capacity-building in terms of increasing access to the Internet. Using the World Wide Web to connect microlending organizations administratively can help reduce their processing and transactions costs and make microlending more attractive for mainstream commercial banks. Other networks would do well to take a close look at the ways in which microlending networks are taking advantage of the opportunities created by the information revolution.

IMPLEMENTING IDEAS AND DECISIONS

Implementation is a challenge for all networks at some point in their existence. Some GPP networks, however, are designed specifically as implementation mechanisms, typically for inter-governmental treaties that address transboundary problems. The GEF is an example of how the challenges of implementation can provide the momentum for broadening an established network from an intergovernmental to a multisectoral one, in order to effectively close the operational governance gap and deepen participation. The implementation of the Chemical Weapons Convention (CWC) is another example where a trisectoral approach has proved key.

Unlike with the GEF, however, for the CWC it is still an open question whether sufficiently strong mechanisms to allow the participation of all actors can be established.

THE GLOBAL ENVIRONMENT FACILITY

Founded in 1991, the GEF is a hybrid organization, combining a conventional intergovernmental approach with an important network dimension (Box 11). It provides grants for projects in four focal areas: biological diversity, climate change, international waters, and ozone depletion. The GEF is also the financial transfer mechanism for both the 1992 United Nations Framework Convention on Climate Change (UNFCCC) and the 1992 Convention on Biodiversity (CBD), and it provides the funds for economies in transition to meet their commitments under the Montreal Protocol. Since its pilot phase the GEF had been operating on the basis of a more traditional intergovernmental approach, but widespread dissatisfaction among developing countries and criticism by NGOs led to a readjustment of its governance structure in 1994. That restructuring also acknowledged a greater role for NGOs, creating a system of regional focal points to gather their input on the GEF and its council meetings and to disseminate related information on those meetings and on NGO consultations. Finally, the restructured GEF specifically identified NGOs and business entities, along with donors and governments, as eligible to prepare and execute GEF projects.

The business community has only gradually become involved in implementation, with activities ranging from strategic and policy advice on GEF-funded projects to technical input and studies. Several projects engage private firms, industries, and their associations in one or more components. For example, some climate-change projects funded by the GEF involve participation of energy service companies in the delivery and maintenance of electric power systems. The lessons learned from the GEF implementation network can serve as a useful resource for the implementation of other treaties in the global environmental arena (see Chapter 5).

Box 11
The Global Environment Facility

~ The GEF was launched jointly by the UNDP, the UNEP, and the World Bank in 1991, as a financial mechanism to provide grants and other funds to recipient nations for projects and activities with the goal of environmental protection with a global focus;

~ It recognizes as key concerns four issue areas that transcend international borders: global climate change, biological diversity, ozone-layer depletion, and the pollution of water resources;

~ It actively involves NGOs in the execution and planning of more than 200 projects;

~ Through a small grants program (up to $50 000 for national projects and up to $250 000 for regional ones), it provides grass-roots groups with financial support to achieve their environmental goals;

~ It collaborates with private-sector representatives to provide additional financial and technical assistance;

~ It formulates policy through an assembly, a council, and a secretariat;

~ The assembly, which meets every 3 years to review GEF policies, includes representatives from all participating countries;

~ The council, the GEF's governing body, consists of 32 constituencies, which include representatives from all regions of the world;

~ The secretariat ensures the effectiveness of policy decisions, coordinates policy formulation, and oversees the implementation of approved programs;

~ Successful negotiation of institutional arrangements in 1994 resulted in a trust fund of more than $2 billion;

~ The GEF covers the cost difference (or increment) between a project undertaken with global environmental objectives in mind and an alternative project that the country would have implemented in the absence of global environmental concerns;

~ It offers funds to any nation that is eligible to borrow from the World Bank or that has the approval to receive technical grants from the UNDP;

~ It approved more than 116 projects worth $733 million in the pilot phase; and

~ It includes more than 35 nations as donors, with combined commitments in excess of $2.75 billion.

Find out more about the GEF at **www.gefweb.org** on the Internet.

THE CHEMICAL WEAPONS CONVENTION

The CWC (Box 12) is another example of an intergovernmental treaty for which a trisectoral mode of implementation is important. But unlike the GEF, where the focus is on project-financing and capacity-building, a trisectoral approach is indispensable as an in-built knowledge-management mechanism to ensure that the CWC

Box 12
The Chemical Weapons Convention

~ The CWC prohibits the development, production, acquisition, stockpiling, retention, transfer, and use of chemical weapons;

~ It was opened for signature in January 1993 and entered into force in April 1997;

~ It is the first disarmament agreement negotiated in a multilateral framework that provides for the elimination of an entire category of weapons under universal international control;

~ It is also a network formally initiated by representatives of the public sector, including the military, the intelligence community, and nations that supported the improvement of relations between the United States and the former Soviet Union;

~ Private-sector representatives were encouraged to assist in the network because of the possibility of increased costs, further regulation, and damage from public outcry;

~ Stakeholders in civil society such as NGOs and scientists have played a key role in bringing new information and ideas about chemical weapons control to the public sector;

~ The Pugwash Conferences, an annual gathering of scientists concerned with the development of weapons of mass destruction, has acted as the most important civil catalyst for the CWC;

~ The structure of the Pugwash Conferences offers selected individuals (advisers to governments, experts in the academic field, and others) an opportunity to express their views in a confidential and informal setting;

~ Pugwash resulted in the inclusion of research institutions such as the Stockholm International Peace Research Institute in Sweden and the Midwest Research Institute of Kansas City in the United States, which produced a succession of papers that were then transmitted to various disarmament delegations. Guidelines for on-site inspections were established with the joint cooperation of research institutions and several representatives from the private sector. The Organization for the Prohibition of Chemical Weapons has a budget of $65 million for 2000.

For more about the CWC visit **www.opcw.nl** on the Internet.

machinery is keeping up with scientific advances and technological change in the chemicals industry. As Emmanuelle Tuerlings and Julian Robinson point out in their case study, the public sector alone cannot be charged with the sourcing of information on scientific advances. National authorities have more than enough to do to simply discharge their routine duties within the control schedules. They may not always have the time or the capabilities to look beyond the schedules into what is happening in the research laboratories.

Responding to this problem, CWC members established both an International Scientific Advisory Board (ISAB) and advisory bodies for their national authorities. The membership of these advisory bodies, on which a heavy burden has been laid by default, is not drawn solely or even mainly from the public sector. It is drawn also from business and civil society: the chemical industry, universities, and the professional community. Indeed, a number of the individuals concerned also belong to Pugwash, an international movement of concerned scientists. Ideally, these national advisory boards and ISAB would form a central part of a CWC implementation network. Unfortunately, however, the participation of civil-society actors is seriously curtailed by provisions in the treaty that prescribe secrecy and confidentiality. Because a balance has to be found between transparency and confidentiality, a mechanism is also needed to give civil society sufficient access to relevant information. If the balance is skewed toward confidentiality, civil society will not have access to relevant information and a trisectoral implementation network will not be able to develop around the CWC.

CLOSING THE PARTICIPATORY GAP

Although the cases described thus far include some where trisectoral global networks provide what economists refer to as global public goods, they go far beyond just delivering a product. Following established practice in domestic public policy, GPP networks also engage in a process of determining what is or is not in the broader global public interest. Within this process, networks raise the profile of an issue to the point where addressing it comes to be considered in the global public interest. Networks also typically go on to explore options for meeting that interest in the most efficient, effective, and participatory manner. Recognition of this process dimension of networks leads us to a broader discussion of the informal and intangible outcomes that trisectoral networks often generate.

By initiating a transnational policy discourse, GPP networks respond to the participatory gap in international decision-making. Successful GPP networks facilitate social interaction among people and organizations that in many cases had almost exclusively been working against each other. To use Robert Putnam's terminology, networks of "civic engagement" allow dilemmas of collective action to be resolved by fostering norms of generalized reciprocity and the emergence of trust, building what one might call global social capital. The notion of global social capital points to the possibility that GPP networks may, at least in the medium or long term, help in creating such trust across national boundaries. In so doing they would facilitate the formation of social capital, not only within societies and single sectors, but also across societies, which is critical for constituting a global public space.

This is a crucial precondition not just for consensus-building and cooperation but also for the functioning of markets. In many cases, the initiation of GPP networks, such as the WCD, turns out to be an investment in social capital that, despite some initial costs, pays off in the long run. As described above, the WCD negotiation process was jointly initiated by the World Bank and the IUCN. With no early guarantee of success, the two organizations funded the first step of the WCD process, the conference in Gland, Switzerland. This was an investment in a long-term process that was widely regarded as very difficult and unpromising. It soon turned out, however, that the careful initiation of a trisectoral approach was generating rewards: it was creating a sense of trust and reciprocal understanding among the various sectors, paving the way for later agreement. Whether the trust thereby created will be sufficient to see the organization through the later implementation phase remains to be seen, however. Interestingly, the participatory approach chosen for the process of setting standards for large-dam construction was diffused to the regional and local levels: the WCD initiated a series of regional hearings and case studies on dam construction and offered a multi-sectoral approach for doing this. In this way the WCD introduced transparent and stakeholder-oriented decision-making processes at the local, regional, and national levels that may well be replicated in other public-policy domains.

An example of underinvestment in a policy process and in social capital is the failure of the MAI, as Katia Tieleman argues in her case study. The Organisation for Economic Co-operation and Development (OECD), as the international organization sponsoring the investment treaty, simply did not get the process right. NGOs felt left out of the process, and business was not sufficiently interested or motivated to participate. After initial criticism of the secretive and exclusionary negotiation process, the OECD responded by doing too little, too late. As opposition to the treaty grew, every prospect for reconciliation and cooperation between the OECD and civil-society organizations was shattered, thanks to tone-deaf public officials and overly radical NGOs. This episode demonstrates that getting the process right is a critical precondition for making policy processes inclusive, legitimate, and sustainable.

TI, whose experience was discussed above, is an example of a network that succeeded in building trust between various sectors and in enabling actors to learn. Corruption was widely regarded, at least until the mid-1990s, as a topic that was "too hot to handle." States as well as international organizations either studiously ignored its existence or neglected to take the steps needed to counter it. In fact, some countries, developed and developing alike, provided (and in many cases still provide) incentives for corruption by offering tax breaks to their corporations that bribe foreign officials. However, since the early 1990s corruption has come to be increasingly under-stood as a major impediment to development, governance, and the legitimacy of democratic institutions.

It was TI that successfully placed the issue of corruption on the global agenda and on the agendas of many individual countries as well. TI was also able to forge national and trisectoral coalitions to work against corruption — a process that presupposes a substantial amount of trust between the various participants. As Fredrik Galtung remarks in his case study, TI serves as a "bridging alliance between such unlikely parties as the World Bank and women's groups in Ugandan villages, and the OECD countries and investigative journalists in Russia." TI chose a nonadversarial strategy that eschewed investigation and exposure of corrupt practices and instead focused on cooperation, encouragement, consultation, education, and personal influence. TI accumulates and harbours high-quality knowledge and expertise on issues related to corruption. This expertise, combined with the high credibility of TI's leadership, has contributed to the emergence of relationships based on trust between TI itself, businesses, states, and international organizations. In forging these trisectoral coalitions, TI not only works against corruption but also engages in capacity-building, by enabling local communities, especially in developing countries, to take democratic control over their destinies. Specifically, TI supplies instruments for such learning, for instance its Integrity Pact or the mutually agreed upon Code of Conduct. The fight against corruption, although having quite tangible outcomes, thus also generates intangible gains, such as greater learning in local communities, firms, and bureaucracies. In the course of its work, TI has also built up a very good reputation for itself, and the coalitions against corruption it has initiated and sponsored have contributed to the creation of trust between the very diverse actors in this sensitive issue area.

Intangible outcomes should not be overlooked when measuring the performance of networks and evaluating their outputs. They are critical to sustaining globalization, for they ensure that a growing number of public-policy decisions are embedded in frameworks in which the most basic elements of participatory governance are present. These functions of GPP networks deserve more attention, because "getting the process right" is of crucial importance for the ultimate success of public-policy-making.

As this chapter has shown, GPP networks can perform a wide variety of functions, both confronting the challenges and taking advantage of the opportunities outlined in Chapter 2. Some critical issues have already been highlighted, for example, the significance of intangible outcomes, as well as the importance of regular review mechanisms and clear and focused goals. The next chapter will explore these lessons in more detail and present a set of critically important issues for successful network management.

Chapter 4

NETWORK MANAGEMENT

What does it take to make networks tick? There are no simple recipes. As the previous chapter demonstrated, networks appear to be situational and opportunistic, and network dynamics cannot be managed mechanistically. Networks do, however, respond to management that emphasizes skilful social entrepreneurship, internal flexibility, and the ability to learn fast. One can distil some further general lessons about how best to manage a network process. But network managers first need to understand that it is seldom they that need to develop the solutions that their networks seek — more often, it is the stakeholders themselves. Rather, the goal of a network manager is to manage the tensions and conflicts that inevitably arise from a committed search for solutions to real problems, and it is up to the network manager to do this in a constructive manner that keeps participants engaged. Although the list is by no means exhaustive, crucial management issues include the following:

+∾+ Getting the network off the ground through leadership and the creation of a common vision;

+∾+ Balancing adequate consultation and goal delivery;

+∾+ Securing sustainable funding (because money talks);

+∾+ Maintaining the "structure" in structured informality;

+∾+ Finding allies outside one's sector; and

+∾+ Tackling the dual challenge of inclusion (North–South and local–global).

GETTING THE NETWORK OFF THE GROUND

Both individual and institutional leadership are central to getting a network up and running. Through the power of their vision, social entrepreneurs can bring the relevant actors together and persuade them to throw their weight behind an issue. The chair of the WCD, Kadar Asmal, contributed greatly to enhancing the respectability and legitimacy of that organization. Asmal offered impeccable moral credentials: one World Bank manager described him as "an individual with courage, commitment, and moral authority." Although Asmal was not immune to criticism from various stakeholders, his expertise and experience muted any efforts to block his selection for the chair, and his leadership proved crucial in getting the various sectors together.

The leadership role played by US Secretary of Labor Robert Reich in initiating the AIP went beyond that of a policy entrepreneur seizing on an issue at a crucial juncture. Reich acted as an agent provocateur, goading the apparel industry into negotiations with NGOs and organized labour. During those negotiations, members of the socially responsible investment community and religious leaders played a significant role by raising the public profile of the sweatshop issue and thus helping to keep pressure on the apparel companies. But without Reich's energy or the endorsement of the White House, the AIP's efforts would have lacked credibility. Given the US domestic political environment at the time, it was clear that the partnership could only go forward as a voluntary effort between business and the NGOs. The US government therefore limited its role to that of facilitator and cheerleader, but Reich took on that role with gusto.

The success of the negotiation of the Ottawa Convention cannot be separated from the leadership demonstrated by Canada's Foreign Affairs Minister Lloyd Axworthy and by Jody Williams, coordinator of the ICBL. Perceiving the stalemate in the formal UN process to revise the 1980 Convention on Certain Conventional Weapons, Axworthy jump-started a new process with a very simple and clear objective: to get a treaty for a comprehensive ban on landmines signed within 14 months. For her part, Williams made a critical contribution by keeping the international campaign focused and maintaining a constant flow of information among its members.

Often, institutional leadership complements and sustains the efforts of individuals. In the case of the RBM initiative, WHO exercised institutional leadership to get the network off the ground. This case also illustrates that leadership does not come on the cheap — it requires internal adjustment and change on the part of the lead institution and its collaborators. Institutional leadership also requires committed individuals at the top, such as Gro Harlem Brundtland, Director of WHO. Having provided the initial leadership and initiative to bring researchers and existing networks on malaria eradication together, WHO remains an important actor in the RBM network. Among other tasks, it is charged with providing strategic direction for the network and serving as a catalyst for action, working to build and sustain country and global partnerships, and ensuring that all aspects of RBM's activities are appropriately monitored.

Although actual implementation has not yet started, the biggest problem facing the RBM network in general and its leadership in particular is the transformation of its organizational culture away from one based on vertical (push) initiatives toward one relying on sector-wide (pull) approaches. The problem of moving beyond business as usual is encountered not only in organizations like WHO but also in individual donor countries and their organizations and in the malaria-affected countries themselves. The success of the RBM initiative will depend on whether WHO can transform itself from within and educate other actors. It remains to be seen whether WHO will be able to continue playing the role of leader of RBM while transforming itself into a team player in a GPP network. The sustainability of the network will also depend on whether or not WHO tries to usurp the credit for possible success.

Leadership has to focus on getting the network dynamics right from the start. Two issues are of utmost importance: getting the right people on board and creating a common vision. Selecting the right mix and number of participants for the early meetings is crucial because they can work as "multipliers," attracting other interested parties to come on board. The WCD Forum, for example, is a group of about 60 representatives from the most important stakeholder groups and organizations in the WCD. It acts as a sounding board for the WCD process but also as a networking mechanism in itself. It is a crucial vehicle for the outreach activities of the commission and for mobilizing other actors that are not formal participants of the WCD process but still may have a strong interest in the commission's work. The WCD Forum will also most likely play a crucial role in disseminating the results of the WCD's work and in helping to execute follow-up activities. Its experience shows that it is important to have representatives of the most important groups and sectors on board but that it is also essential not to expand the number of participants too quickly.

Network leaders also have to make sure that participants realize that they depend on each other to solve the problem and must think innovatively about how best to address the challenge at hand. A "vision exercise" at the beginning of the process may be essential for developing common goals. The experience of both the WCD and the Global Water Partnership (GWP) (Box 13) underlines this point. Both networks started out with informal workshops in which

---

Box 13
The Global Water Partnership

~ The GWP was initiated in the aftermath of two 1992 conferences, on water and the environment (in Dublin and Rio de Janeiro, respectively), where participants identified the need to coordinate efforts in the management and development of water resources;

~ It brings together international organizations, local businesses, and NGOs to foster innovative and, especially, participatory forms of governance in water management;

~ It is an informal institution with a regionally self-reliant system that emphasizes the participation of leading stakeholders within the regions;

~ It encourages participants to use the network's resources to acquire information about the experiences and needs of other parties;

~ It provides strategic assistance in an informal, self-reliant way through regional technical advisory committees;

~ It involves its committees in the creation of regional institutions, policy formulation and analysis, and long-term capacity-building;

~ It includes as donors Australia, Canada, Denmark, France, the Netherlands, Norway, Sweden, Switzerland, the United Kingdom, the UNDP, and the World Bank; and

~ It has a projected budget of $9.04 million for 2000.

Find out more about the GWP at **www.gwp.sida.se** on the Internet.

participants were able to formulate goals free from the pressures of the usual institutional environment. These exercises are often a crucial tool for the development of trust between participants who previously had been working against each other or at cross-purposes. They can only succeed, however, if participants are willing to question their own well-trodden ways of thinking — they have to "leave their institutional boxes," as one experienced networker put it. This is how one creates the social "glue" that makes actors work together on an ongoing basis, engendering the sense of ownership and commitment that help to sustain the network.

Of course, vision exercises are no panacea for managing the often dissonant expectations of participants. The case of the GWP shows that, after the initial meetings, these differences in expectations persist. Some see the network as an action mechanism, others as a mere forum for information exchange. Some favour a facilitating role; others, a hard-core financing role. Some favour thematic priorities; others, regional priorities. Managing these diverse expectations is key to the network's success — and an important challenge for its leadership.

Leadership, individual and institutional alike, can even turn into a liability if a network becomes too closely tied to a single individual or institution. Once the network has passed the initial hurdles and established itself as a leading voice in raising awareness on a global issue, its social entrepreneurs must be ready to share their power in the network as they recruit vital constituents from all three sectors. This form of "leading from behind" has also proved successful in other institutional contexts. By acting as convenors and providing seed money, the IUCN and the World Bank acted as the main drivers in the early stages of the WCD, only to withdraw from their central role later. Thus, the roles of individuals and organizations in a network can change over time. Indeed, there is good reason to believe that both the IUCN and the World Bank will be actively involved in the implementation of standards developed through the WCD process.

BALANCING ADEQUATE CONSULTATION AND GOAL DELIVERY

A central challenge that all participants in networks face is how best to combine balanced consultation with timely delivery on the network's objectives. On the one hand, networks by their nonhierarchical nature thrive on extensive but time-consuming consultation processes. On the other hand, network participants are under pressure from their constituencies to deliver results. Every network has to find ways of getting the process right while still getting the product out the door.

It is important to allow for extensive consultations, especially in the start-up phase of a network. Once a decision to launch a network has been made, establishing its legitimacy requires broad and representative inclusion, and this comes at the risk of delay in making decisions. A focus on process management must adroitly manage expectations. Network sponsors, observers, and critics alike must be reminded that it is not just the tangible outcomes that are important. Intangible outcomes also matter, as does the process by which both kinds of outcomes are achieved. Indeed the "right" process is an important precondition for any tangible outcomes to materialize. That said, however, there is always a danger of getting trapped in the process. A talk shop that fails to generate visible benefits within a set time frame will not last long. That is why networks must establish clear and measurable objectives on a preset timetable, even if some of those objectives seem insignificant or set up as "easy wins."

The Global Alliance for Vaccines and Immunization (GAVI) used what the organization calls milestones to monitor its progress and keep the network focused (Box 14). GAVI has a very broad mandate: to fulfill the right of every child to be protected against vaccine-preventable diseases. This mission requires a bold and sustained institutional effort, for which a trisectoral network that brings together international organizations, civil society, and private industry seems well suited. However, as we have already seen, networks do have comparatively high start-up costs and seldom produce immediate results. This may both alienate donors and put partnerships at risk, as over time participants lose sight of the specific goals. Clearly defined milestones are thus crucial for sustaining long-term

---

Box 14
The Global Alliance for Vaccines and Immunization

~ GAVI seeks to improve access to immunization services, promote vaccination as an integral part of public health systems, and accelerate the development of new vaccines;

~ It receives guidance from a governing board of several international stake-holders, developing-country delegates, representatives of the business community, bilateral agencies, and other associates, who jointly determine objectives and strategies;

~ It has set up three task-force teams, of limited duration, to address global immunization issues:

  – Through its country-coordination task force, it identifies best practices for establishing organizational systems and pilot programs within selected countries,

  – Through its advocacy task force, it articulates a common vision among member agencies and the global immunization community, and

  – Through its task force on financing, it identifies affordable strategies to improve the vaccination capabilities of the world's poorest nations;

~ It is run by a small secretariat, based at the United Nations Children's Fund (UNICEF), which implements the decisions of the governing board; and

~ It receives funding from UNICEF, WHO, the World Bank, the PATH-CVP and Bill and Melinda Gates Children's Vaccine Program, the Rockefeller Foundation, the International Federation of Pharmaceutical Manufacturers Associations, and other organizations (each partner contributes $300 000 to the budget each year).

Visit the UNICEF webpage at **www.unicef.org** on the Internet to learn more about GAVI and related initiatives.

---

support from donors and keeping all participants on board. They keep the network participants focused on the short- and medium-term operational goals of the network, and they provide proof to donors that the network is producing tangible outcomes and is not getting trapped in process.

Moreover, by selecting interim goals that are "easy wins," networks can deliver results fairly early on and thus gain legitimacy with their constituencies (especially their financiers). In the case of the GWP, an easy success in a cooperation project in Africa fostered the network's legitimacy. If no easy win can be identified, other strategies for generating early results must be adopted. One such strategy is to focus, first, on narrow, specific, and technical dimensions of a larger problem domain. Delivering early results supports the reputation of a network, giving it breathing room to run in parallel the more time-consuming consultative processes that will deliver important intangible outcomes and create the trust that is a critical precondition for eventual success.

SECURING SUSTAINABLE FUNDING

How a network obtains its financial support is vital for its credibility and sustainability. Although seed money for a network can come from a single source, trisectoral financial support can be important when the network's primary purpose is consensus-building. To preserve its credibility, the WCD distributes its funding responsibilities among government agencies, multilateral organizations, and business associations, as well as NGOs and foundations. More important, no single donor from any sector contributes more than 10% of the group's budget. This rule has proved crucial for ensuring the WCD's independence, but it comes at a cost: fund-raising is much more difficult when one must accumulate a number of fairly small contributions. The time and resources that the WCD had to devote to fund-raising initially hampered its capacity to do its broader work.

Truly trisectoral funding arrangements can be less important for networks whose primary purpose is implementation. The GEF, for example, whose legitimacy is linked to formal intergovernmental treaties, is financed mainly by a single source: governments. It has only slowly expanded its sources of funding to include the private sector. Given the less conflictual nature of the GEF process, a trisectoral funding arrangement is of less importance. To take another example, CGIAR is financed primarily by the contributions of members, which include states, foundations, and international organizations. As Curtis Farrar shows in his case study, industrial countries (specifically, the members of the Development Assistance Committee of the OECD) account for more than two-thirds of CGIAR financing. Membership in CGIAR is open to nonprofit entities that accept its goals and agree to contribute resources of at least $500 000. CGIAR recognizes private companies as stakeholders but does not accept them as members because of the potential for perceived conflicts of interest. CGIAR research centres, however, welcome contributions of funds from this source.

Rugmark, an international program to combat and prevent the use of child labour in carpet-making in South Asia, provides a good example of an innovative approach to financing a network. The initiative includes independent, external, on-site production-monitoring of carpet producers; carpets may display the Rugmark label if they are certified as having been produced without child labour. Monitors are hired and trained by the Rugmark Foundation. Carpet producers applying for a licence bind themselves to not employing children under 14 years of age and to paying general wages according to local legal minimum-wage requirements. Family producers have to prove that their children go to school. Carpet-producing companies have to provide the Foundation with full information about their production sites, which are then regularly inspected by full-time inspectors. European and American importers of labeled carpets pay 1% of the import value of the carpet. The funds generated through the sale of Rugmark-labeled carpets are in turn channeled into programs providing social rehabilitation and education for children in the affected regions. This is done to avoid pressing former child weavers back into illegal employment and to provide them with a minimum education. Regular reports are issued on the use of these funds. Transparency of funding is essential to ensuring the network's accountability.

It is also critical that funding be sustained for at least a few years — a difficult task, especially for trisectoral networks that evolve around consensus-building. After all, the real strength and value added of these networks rest on the fact that they do not claim to offer a solu-tion at their inception but provide an environment for stakeholders to develop solutions. Thus, apart from such intangible outcomes as trust, many networks cannot and should not guarantee success. But this "no-guarantees" approach exposes the providers of funding to financial risk. One way to reduce that risk is to establish a strict time limit for the initiative. As discussed in Chapter 3, the WCD has done just that: the organization is set to dissolve in June 2000. Another, less restrictive approach could establish an independent external review that assesses the accomplishments of the network after a given period of time and makes recommendations for further action. The GEF is one network that has changed its setup considerably following the recommendations of an external review (see below).

MAINTAINING THE "STRUCTURE" IN STRUCTURED INFORMALITY

The right institutional setup is critical to ensure that networks keep their "structured informality" and are able to deliver what they promise. Networks have to avoid falling into the trap of becoming just another institution. This means they must avoid building up bureaucracies and must put rigorous review processes in place. Successful networks build on existing institutions to the extent possible and limit their own secretariats to a minimum. This is a lesson learned from the secretariat of the HIV–AIDS network. During the 1980s that organization developed largely into an agency of its own, and this invited participating agencies and partners to ease up on their own efforts, knowing they could rely on the services of the secretariat. The GAVI Secretariat, in contrast, restricts its activities to pure coordination and minimizing competition for operational activities, by allowing partners to choose their areas of engagement according to their own relative strength.

Built-in review processes are critical to preserving a network's character as a learning organization and to preventing ossification of structures, practices, and people. In addition to permanent internal review processes (for example, comparing achievements against goals and milestones set earlier), regular external reviews are essential. The GEF has gone through two extensive, independent review processes, both of which made important suggestions for restructuring the institution. These reviews are critical because, as one GEF official put it, "We don't know what the road looks like, what the drivers and roadblocks will be, [so] it is important to have an evolving flexible partnership." CGIAR has also carried out three system-wide reviews and other cross-cutting studies. Yet, important as such reviews are, equally important is allowing for learning on a day-to-day basis, and this means keeping networks open to an exchange of views and receptive to outside opinions.

FINDING ALLIES OUTSIDE ONE'S SECTOR

To move network processes forward, it is often useful to look for alliances across the three sectors. Sectors, after all, are not monolithic, and sometimes intrasectoral divides create opportunities for innovative intersectoral networking.

Greenpeace's initiative in the case of the UNFCCC exemplifies how drawing in new actors can make a crucial difference to the public-policy-making process. As Paul Hohnen argues in his case study, Greenpeace was able to achieve a coup in international climate-change negotiations by engaging private insurance companies and motivating them to speak out. For Greenpeace, seeking allies in the business community was important, because the group needed their expertise to speak more authoritatively on the risks of global warming, using independent analysis of the potential costs of climate change. Some insurance companies had already started evaluating the impact of climate change and assessing the risks for their business; hence, they were suitable partners for Greenpeace in the climate-change debate. Some major insurance companies had come to understand the danger that climate change posed for their business, and some of their independent research studies confirmed the findings of Greenpeace and others on the sources and effects of climate change. Soon a number of the largest insurance companies started to take a public profile on the issue, calling for governments to take "urgent and dramatic measures."

To what extent the influence of the insurance industry was a determining factor in the final decisions made at the Kyoto negotiations remains unclear. Although it might not have had more than a catalytic effect, there is no doubt that Greenpeace's strategy of seeking unlikely allies from various sectors helped to spur a slow negotiation process and build a broader coalition for change. By bringing in the insurance industry, Greenpeace was able to tip the balance of power within the negotiations by exploiting intrasectoral differences between the fossil-fuel and insurance industries.

As in the case of Greenpeace and the insurance industry, with the AIP, intrasectoral differences have played an important role in moving the agenda. At first sight, the AIP is an unlikely alliance.

Why did certain parts of the business community and certain parts of civil society (most notably, NGOs and, initially, the labour unions) decide to collaborate on the issue of sweatshops, whereas others stayed away? First, although parts of the apparel industry were clearly reluctant to go public and acknowledge that sweatshops are a problem, others saw the initiative as a welcome opportunity to improve their public image or show that they already had implemented far-reaching improvements in working conditions. Second, within civil society, organized labour and some NGOs were unenthusiastic from the start about setting voluntary codes of conduct and networking with the business community. By choosing to collaborate with some influential but less sceptical NGOs, the US government and the participating business community were able to forge new coalitions, which later drew in other participants from these sectors as well. Currently, the AIP is about to enter its implementation phase, where it faces some critical new challenges, as discussed in Chapter 3. Although it seems premature to speculate about the AIP's future, some of the lessons learned from other networks that have successfully managed the transition from negotiation to implementation may be instructive for the key players. The lessons learned about sustained leadership and network management, discussed above, may prove particularly relevant.

Intrasectoral divisions can also be exploited in the public domain, as the landmines case demonstrates. In the early phase, the Ottawa process was a de facto alliance among certain governments, the ICBL, and certain UN agencies. As Ann Peters argues in her case study, dissatisfaction over the limitations of the 1980 Convention on Certain Conventional Weapons, together with the results of a review conference 15 years later, led to a "division among governments on the issue of a comprehensive ban on anti-personnel weapons and fostered firmer links between particular governments and non-governmental organizations." This alliance managed to marginalize obstructionist governments and move the process forward from a stalemated intergovernmental process at the United Nations.

The moderate wing of the debt-relief movement has also explicitly sought allies outside its own sector. What started as an advocacy coalition among NGOs and church groups has developed into a loose network of civil-society, intergovernmental, and state actors. There have been explicit attempts by activists to dialogue with officials of creditor and debtor governments and the international financial institutions (IFIs), and similarly these officials have initiated meetings with civil-society groups. Moderate Group of Seven leaders and IFI officials have expressed limited support for Jubilee 2000 campaign demands. As a result, these actors have been brought into the broader network of debate, if not consensus, on the issue. Although some network actors continue to view government and IFI officials as targets, many are starting to think of them as partners in the effort to relieve the debt of many poor countries.

TACKLING THE DUAL CHALLENGE OF INCLUSION

Although often described as global, most public-policy networks are in fact dominated by elite actors (public and private) from the industrial world, with few ties to developing-country groups or local institutions. Many networks exist in a wholly global space, made up of intergovernmental bodies, multinational corporations, and transnational "mega-NGOs." Within each sector, divisions exist between these bodies, mostly headquartered in developed countries, and their local counterparts, especially those in developing countries. The ability of networks to achieve their long-term goals, however, is influenced by their willingness and capacity to involve such counterparts. These two dimensions — North versus South, and local versus global — constitute the dual challenge of inclusion.

After discussing the importance of inclusion for networking processes, this section presents various strategies that networks have employed to address the inclusion challenge. "Local" here is conceptualized broadly to include all civil-society organizations, businesses, and governments that are not global in their orientation; in other words, local organizations for the purposes of this report are those that are territorially bound in any way. National, state, and provincial governments fall within this category, as do nontransnational businesses and many grass-roots NGOs.

The level of involvement of local and developing-country participants in networks can vary throughout the policy cycle.

Many networks seek to address issues of particular concern in developing countries (such as malaria, landmines, debt relief, and microlending), and so they rely on data and information gathered in those countries during the initiation stage. Later on, however, the local suppliers of this information are generally excluded from the policy negotiation stage because they are assumed (rightly or wrongly) to be represented by their governments or by elements of civil society. As a result, many networks do not seek widespread participation by local actors until many of the most difficult decisions have already been made. Often, the only reason for bringing local actors back in is to make sure that the policies chosen can be implemented on the ground.

This limited participation by local and developing-country actors has led to criticism of the global public-policy-making process. Critics blame networks for trying to impose developed-country norms and values on developing countries. A recent editorial in the South Centre's newsletter, for example, charged that networks, particularly those focused on economic issues, are being used to extend capitalist domination abroad. In this context, the debt-relief movement has been divided between reformists and radicals over whether donors should require market-focused economic reforms for poor countries to become eligible. Representatives of both viewpoints can be found in both the North and the South, although the more radical voices are stronger in developing countries. Similarly, networks are criticized for trying to impose global norms within the field of human rights. Although opponents often invoke cultural arguments simply as a way to resist change, their claims do raise questions as to whether global norms actually exist in some issue areas.

Critics also sometimes accuse networks dominated by industrial countries of seeking to prevent developing countries from developing. In the CWC negotiations, for example, developing countries worried that the industrial countries would limit technology transfers to the developing world because the dual-use nature of some sensitive technologies (that is, their ability to be used in weapons as well as for peaceful purposes) posed a security threat. Consensus was ultimately achieved by including in the accord a passage acknowledging the economic and technological development needs of these countries.

Finally, and this is related to the previous point, networks are sometimes accused of trying to enforce double standards. Many environmental efforts have been criticized for unfairly imposing costs on developing countries when it is the industrialized countries that have been the main contributors to the problem. Think, for example, of the debate surrounding the ban of chlorofluorocarbons (CFCs), a group of chemicals that contribute to the depletion of the ozone layer. As Reiner Grundmann describes in his case study, some countries, such as China and India, saw the Montreal Protocol, to regulate the reduction of CFCs, as inequitable and refused to sign. Although their own CFC production at that time was minimal, under the protocol it was assumed that China and India would absorb 30% of total world production by 2000. Both countries demanded adequate financial support and clearly defined access to alternative technologies before they would sign the protocol (see below).

WHY INCLUSION MATTERS

Inclusion of diverse groups in a networking process is important for several reasons. First, the active participation of local and developing-country actors gives legitimacy to global policies and demonstrates that those policies have not been derived in a global vacuum but reflect real concerns on the ground. As we have already seen, networks that lack such inclusion are often subjected to sharp criticism. Accusations that networks impose industrial-country values, prevent development, and enforce double standards all serve to question the legitimacy of both the process and its outcomes. As long as there are vocal people making such charges, the "global" nature of the network in question will remain in doubt. In addition, the extent to which networks are somehow accountable to public opinion depends on the nature of these links with local groups in countries around the world. Inclusion therefore fosters both network legitimacy and accountability by allowing more people to have a say in shaping policy outcomes.

As Timothy Sisk writes in his case study,

> *One of the principal lessons learned from the democracy promotion field is that local actors need to be more fully and systematically included in the GPP network if external assistance for democracy promotion is to be more successful.*

Local participation brings legitimacy to the process, particularly in issue areas where global networks may be viewed as interventionist or seen as a source of interference in internal affairs.

Second, public-policy decisions, however global in their reach, ultimately must be implemented on the ground. Local people and institutions must therefore be on board right from the start if they are to be expected to carry out network goals and sustain them over the long term. As we know from the recent debate on the effectiveness of foreign aid, the success of a project depends upon securing the commitment of stakeholders to implement it. A sense of local ownership also increases the likelihood that policies will be sustainable after the donors have gone home. Success in networks responds to the same logic. This commitment can be achieved by encouraging stakeholders to take ownership of the network through participation in all stages of the policy cycle, from planning through to implementation. The example of forest management shows how crucial the inclusion of local actors is, especially during the implementation stage. Both the Intergovernmental Panel on Forests (IPF) and its successor, the Intergovernmental Forum on Forests (IFF), have so far failed to establish a link back to the local level. As Astrid Harnisch demonstrates in her case study, this lack of implementation at the regional and local levels is a prime cause for the problems and insufficiencies of the IPF–IFF process.

Third, inclusion is important from a normative perspective. The premise behind the network approach is that many GPP issues can no longer be addressed through conventional structures, such as intergovernmental organizations. Just as people in countries around the world are demanding a voice in their domestic policy-making processes, so, too, are they seeking to be heard when policy decisions require a global approach. Ultimately, the new institutions of global governance will be sustainable over the long run only if they foster venues for participation and democratic decision-making. This of course is not just a normative question but also a very practical one.

Finally, although we have seen that the operational and normative justifications for broad-based inclusion are compelling, there may be times when widespread participation in a network is not necessary. Certain scientific research networks, for example, seek to keep their work as focused and objective as possible by limiting the involvement of nonscientists. CGIAR has received funding from a wide range of sources and welcomes a broad group of stakeholders, but one of the pillars of its structure is to keep the core network activity — agricultural research — in the control of independent centres where scientists have a predominant role in management. There might be situations where inclusion and in-depth delibera- tion are redundant, simply because the issues involved are not as controversial as, say, those in labour standards. Nevertheless, even networks in these less contentious areas have to maintain an open governance structure and ensure sufficient transparency, just in case new issues of a more conflictual nature are someday put on their agenda. In the case of CGIAR, this point has current relevance: the genetic modification of foodstuffs has already become an important topic on CGIAR's agenda and will certainly trigger a contentious debate. In addition, as Chapter 2 has shown, some older issues might give rise to new conflicts as scientific advances reveal previ- ously unknown side effects or linkages. Therefore, governance structures need to remain flexible and open to accommodate such increasing complexity in knowledge and perceptions.

There are other cases where the inclusion of local groups, at least in the early stages of a network, could actually be risky for those groups. Activism on issues such as internal displacement and the use of child soldiers may threaten many governments. For this reason, the network on internal displacement sought first to develop guiding principles at the global level before seeking local partners. The International Coalition to Stop the Use of Child Soldiers followed a similar track and provided external legitimacy for action by local groups that would otherwise have been risky.

STRATEGIES FOR INCLUSION

A review of the networks analyzed for this report reveals a variety of strategies for including both local and developing-country groups. Some of these strategies have been successful, whereas others have not.

DEFINING AND PURSUING MULTIPLE LEVELS OF ENGAGEMENT

Several networks have sought to incorporate views and opinions from developing countries and local interested parties by bringing the networks closer to them. They have established methods of consultation at the regional, national, and provincial levels. One way this has been done is by establishing national-level organizations whose negotiations and deliberations feed into the global network. The ICBL, for example, served as a communication hub for diverse local NGOs, government officials, and civil-society organizations to become involved in the effort to lobby governments for passage of the Ottawa Convention. It was the combination of pressure from national groups in particular countries drawing their governments' attention to the issue, pressure from several key individuals within the ICBL working on the international level, and country-to-country pressure that accounted for the ultimate success of the landmines campaign.

National delegations also participate in the ISO 14000 negotiations on environmental standards. These delegations have increasingly sought to include local civil-society organizations in their deliberations, with varying success. In some cases, NGOs have not wanted to become involved in a process that is perceived as dominated by industry. The ISO 14000 process has also been less successful at including developing countries, especially those that do not have national standards associations. The involvement of both local and developing-country participants has been hindered by their limited financial and organizational capacity, a problem discussed below.

Another way in which networks have pursued multiple levels of engagement is by holding regional and local consultations during the initiation and negotiation phases. Both the landmines campaign and the International Coalition to Stop the Use of Child Soldiers, for example, held a series of regional conferences at which governments, international organizations, and representatives of civil society were invited to discuss problems and develop regionally appropriate solutions. Organizers emphasized the importance of not reducing the conferences to "coalitions of the like-minded," and the organizers used them as a way to exchange information gathered through in-depth research. In each case, the regional conferences led ultimately to an international meeting at which information and proposals from the regional level were compiled and further negotiated.

The WCD also actively solicited stakeholder views and perspectives through regional consultations and submissions. In addition, the commission initiated a series of local-level research activities: 10 in-depth basin and national case studies, a larger survey of 150 dams around the world, and 17 thematic reviews of cross-cutting issues. The engagement of the network at multiple levels is intended to develop a comprehensive knowledge base, gather ideas from a range of participants, and incorporate stakeholders into the process itself; all of these are deemed crucial to the group's ultimate success.

Finally, some networks conduct their activities at multiple levels, from the local to the global. The informal Global Network for Democracy Promotion has found that a multilayered approach is key to forcing political transition in countries where that is needed. The network features actors from the global level (international donors, UN agencies) to the local level (citizens' groups, in-country activists) that work in formal and informal partnerships on a case-by-case basis. They share resources, knowledge, and experiences from other countries to pressure governments to undergo processes of political liberalization. Although there has been a series of celebrated successes in such countries as El Salvador, Poland, and South Africa, the Global Network for Democracy Promotion has so far failed to bring about true transitions in places like Algeria, Angola, Bosnia, and Burundi.

Similarly, the main function of the UMP is to facilitate city consultations in urban areas around the world. Its process is discussed further below, but it is mentioned here as yet another illustration of bringing networks closer to local and developing-country actors so that they can become more involved.

ESTABLISHING STRUCTURES THAT INSTITUTIONALIZE INCLUSION

Another strategy through which global networks address the challenge of inclusion, particularly of developing countries, is by institutionalizing their participation in network structures. The GEF, for example, has developed a method of representation that is a creative hybrid of the voting systems used in the Bretton Woods institutions (the International Monetary Fund [IMF] and the World Bank) and the United Nations. The system was developed after the GEF's pilot phase, during which a more traditional Bretton Woods-style system of representation was used. The GEF council today comprises representatives from 14 OECD countries, 16 developing countries, and 2 economies in transition. For any measure to pass, it must be approved by votes representing 60% of the countries and 60% of the organization's financial resources. This system gives developing countries greater representation and more power than they have in the Bretton Woods institutions but allows donors more control than they would have through a UN-style, one-country–one-vote mechanism.

Developing countries had little involvement in the establishment of the Montreal Protocol. Some of them took little interest in the process, as both the production of, and the scientific research on, CFCs originated in the industrialized world, and others refused to participate because they saw the process as inequitable. Developing-country participation vastly increased, however, after the establishment of a funding mechanism, known as the Multilateral Fund (MLF), to aid poorer countries in the transition to CFC-free technologies. The MLF is administered by an independent body and managed by a 14-member executive committee, whose representation is split equally between industrial- and developing-country parties to the protocol. This arrangement aims at an equitable distribution of power between rich and poor countries, although donor countries maintain a veto right. In the end, it seems that reductions in emissions of ozone-depleting chemicals in many developing countries were achieved largely through market mechanisms, rather than through the work of the MLF. Nevertheless, the fund was a symbolic victory for the developing world, which helped win global support for the Montreal Protocol (Box 15).

Box 15
The Montreal Protocol

~ The Montreal Protocol was reached in September 1987 with a compromise agreement setting the goal of a 50% cut in production of ozone-depleting substances by 1999;

~ Network participants who were proponents of regulation included scientist advocates, staff members of government agencies and international organizations, and environmental activists;

~ Network members who opposed regulation included (in the 1970s) CFC producers and sceptical scientists and (in the early 1980s) officials of the Reagan administration, the European Community, Japan, and the former Soviet Union;

~ Discovery of the ozone hole over Antarctica in 1985 changed the perception of the problem;

~ The debate was further profoundly affected in 1986, when the Du Pont company, the leading opponent of international standards, perceived regulations as being inevitable;

~ Du Pont changed its position for fear that too obstinate a position might ruin the company's reputation and lead to consumer boycotts;

~ Opponents of regulations were also influenced by the Chernobyl nuclear accident in 1986 and by a policy shift in the German government that influenced several key nations in the European Community;

~ The Montreal Protocol institutionalized a formal structure, with the annual conference of the parties as the highest decision-making body, and with several other governing bodies, including a secretariat, as well as technical, scientific, and socioeconomic working groups; and

~ According to the UNEP, world production of CFCs was cut by half in the period from 1986 to 1992.

For a copy of the provisions outlined in the Montreal Protocol, see **www.unep.org/ozone/mont_t.htm** on the Internet.

In their efforts to institutionalize inclusion, however, networks have to avoid superfluous and rigid governance structures and at the same time integrate a large number of participants from different sectors. As Charlotte Streck writes in her case study on the GEF, the sheer number of actors and agencies involved in that organization led to an overly complicated project cycle and lengthy decision processes. This made it extremely difficult to maintain a structured informality, which is one of the greatest advantages of any network.

GPP networks can also address the dual challenge of inclusion by building on existing efforts at the local level and in developing countries. Several networks have emerged out of grass-roots movements in the developing world. The nascent global network for microcredit, for example, has been building on the experiences and structures of local microlending institutions around the world, the most famous of which is the Grameen Bank in Bangladesh. Similarly, the Rugmark Initiative emerged out of local efforts in South Asia to combat the problem of child labour in rug production. Collaboration with industrial-country partners ultimately led to a system of labeling through which rugs produced without the use of child labour could be identified and marketed.

Opponents of the practice of female genital mutilation have also adopted a grass-roots approach in recent years. After top-down efforts were met with strong criticism for allegedly imposing Western cultural values, industrial-country activists sought to build a network through local groups (including many women's organizations) that were already fighting the practice on the ground. Through this combination of forces, cultural leaders in several communities have been persuaded to ban female genital mutilation.

The RBM initiative also seeks to build on local-level initiatives. Countries where malaria is endemic (primarily in the developing world) are encouraged to develop solid proposals for addressing the problem. During this planning phase, the global network provides countries with the information (and in some cases the guidance) they need to make informed decisions. The resulting country plans are forwarded to international organizations, which are supposed to assist in their implementation. The premise of this sector-wide, client-driven approach is that countries should set their own priorities. Rather than building on vertical initiatives, RBM relies on plans developed at the local level to combat the problem of malaria more effectively.

ADAPTING GLOBAL POLICIES TO LOCAL REALITIES

We have seen how global networks can be built from the bottom up as a way of including a wider array of local and developing-country perspectives. But sometimes the opposite strategy works well: some networks have developed flexible approaches at the global level, which can then be adapted and shaped to fit local realities.

This has been the strategy of the UMP, which supports city consultations in developing countries around the world. This network, based out of the United Nations Centre for Human Settlements (Habitat) in Nairobi, operates through regional offices in Africa, Asia, Latin America, and the Middle East. These regional offices have identified several so-called anchoring institutions — NGOs that identify and work with local partner institutions to facilitate the consultation process. The consultations themselves bring together representatives of the business community, civil society, and government agencies to address urban development problems. This approach has also allowed for the inclusion of traditional cultural authorities, who are often overlooked in other networks. All these stakeholders are prepared through a series of miniconsultations, which introduce program objectives, brief the stakeholders on their roles, and seek to convey local ownership of the process. During the consultation itself, participants concentrate on exchanging information, identifying symbiotic relationships, brainstorming, and selecting a multisectoral committee to draft an action plan. The global network provides policy proposals developed through comparative research and financial resources. The primary contribution of the network, however, is the city consultation process itself, through which those global recommendations can be adapted to reflect local priorities, resources, and creative ideas. In the case of the Travel and Tourism Industry network, annual progress notes based on regional meetings with local-level actors are produced. These progress notes are meant to be merged with Agenda 21 for the travel and tourism industry — the drafting of which was dominated by industrialized-country efforts — to represent the latest thinking on sustainable development.

The notion of developing flexible approaches at the global level that can then be adapted and shaped to fit local realities is more difficult to realize in global standards-setting (discussed below). There a level playing field may be key for the success of a network. Nonetheless, some of the cases discussed in this report illustrate that as long as the desired outcomes are achieved, networks may permit different processes for achieving them.

CAPACITY-BUILDING

A primary obstacle to effective local and developing-country participation in global networks has been their limited financial and organizational capacity. Local and developing-country groups also have less access to basic information than do their transnational counterparts in the industrial countries. This situation is particularly evident with respect to information technology, where the world is becoming increasingly divided between those who have access and those who do not. This division does not line up cleanly along either the local–global or the North–South dimension. Many governments and NGOs in developing countries have access to e-mail and the Internet, whereas many groups in the industrialized world, especially in rural areas and inner cities, do not. On average, though, the South is less "connected" than the North. Regardless, it is clear that grass-roots organizations around the world are limited in the extent to which they can link up with global networks.

Several networks have tried to address this need for capacity-building among local and developing-country partners. RBM, for example, offers direct help and expertise to countries that lack the capacity to develop implementation plans. This network also works through its multilateral members to restructure health-care sectors in affected countries. In the initial phases of the ISO 14000 negotiations, developing-country participation was limited by a lack of technical expertise, financial constraints, and poor access to information. Industrialized states tried to enable developing-country actors (states as well as NGOs) to participate by providing them with financial support, but as discussed in Chapter 3, these efforts fell short.

CGIAR has tried to build the capacity of its collaborators among the national agricultural research centres of developing countries through training and technical advice. One of the 16 centres it supports, the International Service for National Agricultural Research, has the strengthening of national research systems as its principal goal. Nevertheless, given the size of the task and CGIAR's limited resources, the organization has never reached a full consensus on how high a priority to give to this function. Based on this limited range of experiences, it would seem that there is room for more creative strategies to build the capacity of local and developing-country groups to participate in networking.

In general, capacity-building is a long-term process. As many donor agencies and NGOs increasingly recognize, capacity-building activities are most effective when they are demand-driven, that is, determined by the articulated needs of civil-society and state actors themselves, not imposed on them. The case of the RBM network, discussed in Chapter 3, nicely illustrates this approach.

This chapter — based on a review of our cases — has addressed several key managerial challenges that networks face. It is important for international organizations in general and the United Nations in particular to address these challenges.

Chapter 5

NETWORKS AND THE UNITED NATIONS

The world this report has described demands innovative responses to the challenges of global governance, and it has particular implications for the work of the United Nations. The leadership of the United Nations has begun to place the idea of GPP networks at the forefront of its vision and strategy for the UN system so that the organization can more effectively address the challenges facing the world in the 21st century. In his 1999 address to the Annual Meetings of the World Economic Forum, UN Secretary-General Kofi Annan observed the following:

> The United Nations once dealt only with governments. By now we know that peace and prosperity cannot be achieved without partnerships involving governments, international organizations, the business community, and civil society.

Similarly, Mark Malloch Brown, administrator of the UNDP, noted in his foreword to the 1999 *Human Development Report* that

> We are seeing the emergence of a new, much less formal structure of global governance, where governments and partners in civil society, the private sector and others are forming functional coalitions across geographic borders and traditional political lines to move public policy in ways that meet the aspirations of a global citizenry. ... These coalitions use the convening power and the consensus-building, standard-setting and implementing roles of the United Nations, the Bretton Woods institutions and international organizations, but their key strength is that they are bigger than any of us and give new expression to the UN Charter's "We, the peoples."

These statements indicate a clear recognition that for the United Nations to succeed in its mission in the new millennium, it needs to develop a systematic and reliable approach to working together with governments, business, and civil society in GPP networks. Equally important, by facilitating the emergence of these networks and contributing to their effective operation, as well as by strengthening the capacities of states and nonstate actors to participate in GPPs, the United Nations will increase its own effectiveness and credibility. In so doing it will demonstrate to a range of stakeholders and observers, most importantly its clients (member countries), that it is able to support and facilitate the degree of interaction and social learning necessary for GPP networks to succeed.

The Secretary General's Millennium Report — *We, the Peoples: The Role of the United Nations in the 21st Century*, in support of which this publication was written — points out the importance of global public policy networks in redefining the role of the UN:

> *Formal institutional arrangements may often lack the scope, speed and informational capacity to keep up with the rapidly changing global agenda. Mobilizing the skills and other resources of diverse global actors, therefore, may increasingly involve forming loose and temporary global policy networks that cut across national, institutional and disciplinary lines. The United Nations is well situated to nurture such informal "coalitions for change" across our various areas of responsibility.*

The UN's core missions of global peace, sustainable development, and humanitarian relief provide a mandate for the organization to get involved in some of the key global challenges of the 21st century. In addition, given its universal membership, the United Nations is well placed to highlight and address the often neglected but critical challenges of inclusion identified in Chapter 4. Finally, by acting as a facilitator of, and platform for, GPP networks, the United Nations can play an intermediary role between states and business, as well as civil society. Although states' rationale and legitimacy for the foreseeable future will remain constrained by territorial sovereignty, business, which takes advantage of open markets and the technological revolution, has long escaped those constraints.

At the same time, the developments outlined in Chapter 2 have posed a direct challenge to the UN's mission and its ability to respond to today's increasingly complex public-policy issues. Moreover, there are more member states of the United Nations today than ever before, and the economic and informational inequalities between states have increased dramatically, placing the institution's commitment to universalism under strain. Working in and with GPP networks will increasingly be, not just a policy choice, but indeed an operational imperative for the United Nations and its specialized agencies, if it is to meet its own goals effectively and efficiently. In many ways, the future of GPP networks is the future of the United Nations, and vice versa.

This report proposes a three-track approach toward engaging the United Nations in GPP networks. In order for the organization to decide which roles to assume in these networks and how it can coordinate its actions with those of other players, it needs to develop mechanisms of prioritization, coordination, and engagement with private firms and civil society.

FROM VISION TO REALITY: A THREE-TRACK APPROACH

The United Nations does not have to reinvent the wheel to become more engaged in GPP networks. As several of the cases discussed in previous chapters have shown, the United Nations and its specialized agencies are already active in a number of such networks, ranging from technical standards and regulations (International Telecommunication Union, International Civil Aviation Organization, Universal Postal Union, and International Maritime Organization), to sustainable development and human rights (UNEP, WHO, FAO, ILO, UNDP, Office of the United Nations High Commissioner for Human Rights [UNHCHR], and others), to humanitarian relief, refugees, security, disarmament, and political reconstruction (Office of the High Commissioner for Refugees). In some cases, network structures are present in the first two issue areas and less visible, but increasingly important, in the third.

Yet the organization's involvement to date has been piecemeal if not accidental, rather than the result of a deliberate, overarching strategic choice that recognizes the systemic transformation of the international system and considers networks a promising response. Most of these initiatives remain ad hoc and largely at the specialized agency level. UN participation in networks is often uncoordinated across agencies, and there is an absence of a strategic vision that emphasizes selectivity with respect to policy domains and potential roles for the UN system, to ensure maximum leverage and close alignment with its mission. Furthermore, the lessons from these varied experiences among different UN agencies have not been synthesized and analyzed so that others both within the organization and without can learn and best practices can be shared. Lastly, the United Nations has yet to call for a global dialogue with its partner institutions to determine a division of labour that ensures that each institution's comparative advantage is brought to bear in addressing global challenges, ensuring synergies and thus effectiveness and efficiency.

A strategic vision for future engagement of the United Nations in GPP networks has to take into account both the lessons already learned (as presented in the previous chapters) and political realities. The experience of recent reform initiatives and contemporary political realities indicate that there will be no major institutional reforms on the horizon for the United Nations, nor can it expect any major new financial resources. The United Nations faces significant constraints in its political, human, and financial resources and must marshal those limited resources in a strategic manner to leverage change. Building on the lessons learned from our cases and on these political realities, the three-track approach we propose for enhancing UN engagement with GPP networks is at once feasible and visionary:

↝ Strengthen and consolidate existing networks by focusing on implementation and learning processes;

↝ Build implementation networks that will help to revitalize weak or weakening conventions that are important to the UN mission; and

↝ Launch new networks where they are needed.

The emphasis on **strengthening existing GPP networks** concerns those networks whose norms and objectives are clear and have broad support and where the United Nations has comparative advantage in improving inclusiveness and implementation and (or) learning within the network. Strengthening these networks requires a clear and feasible framework for implementation, mechanisms of capacity-building that support inclusiveness and implementation, and the ability of the network to learn from the implementation process. Strengthening GPP networks' abilities to deliver on implementation and learning typically focuses attention on the local–global interaction and shifts the focus away from interaction among and between transnational businesses, international NGOs, and national governments, which tend to dominate the negotiation phase. Networks that have integrated local actors earlier in the policy cycle tend to have fewer problems in implementation, because capacity issues are addressed up front and there is more systematic attention to the local–global dynamic. In the absence of additional financial resources, and given the often delicate political issues involved, the primary emphasis should be on maximizing knowledge resources and creating the most basic information and communications infrastructures, which remain elusive for many.

Chapter 3 touched on the problems of a growing overlap and competition between various initiatives on, for example, codes of conduct, nonbinding auditing procedures, and labels. Competition among these schemes will no doubt allow policymakers to discover their respective strengths and weaknesses. At the same time, how-ever, as previous chapters have shown, the presence of multiple schemes addressing a given issue risks undermining the effort of all of them. UN agencies could help to **consolidate existing initiatives** and develop, in collaboration with other actors, a set of "meta-standards" that would embrace best practices in reporting and auditing procedures, such as social audits or efforts to monitor compliance, and combine them with voluntary initiatives such as codes of conduct. Although such overarching standards run the risk of eliminating the potential for learning that competition entails, the internal learning mechanisms that transparent and inclusive networks contain can compensate for that.

As the GEF has demonstrated, GPP networks can help in the implementation of conventions that are central to the UN's mission. The United Nations could help **build trisectoral implementation networks to revitalize weak or weakening conventions at the core of its mission**, such as the Kyoto Protocol. This would include strengthening pro-reform allies in the business sector (for example, in the insurance and alternative-energy industries), continuing to support scientific and policy research to strengthen the existing transnational research communities (with a selective focus on key countries), and strengthening pro-reform advocacy coalitions between the state and civil society to reduce the divide between North and South.

One dimension of leveraging resources requires the United Nations to act as a network entrepreneur, identifying niches where conditions for **launching new GPP neworks** are ripe, but no one is willing or able to initiate the process, or the process seems to be stalled. Issue areas where such conditions may now exist include genetically modified organisms, fisheries, and transnational crime, including money-laundering. For example, the Secretary General's Millennium Report acknowledges that the issue of biotechnology and genetically modified organisms now demands a broad dialogue amongst a range of stakeholders. That is why the Secretary General calls for a global public policy network to address the risks and opportunities associated with the increased use of biotechnology and bioengineering. Initially such an effort would identify certain specific areas such as food security, where incentive structures have changed in such a way that the prospects for social learning have grown and there are reasons to believe that participants may share a genuine interest in the evolution of consensual knowledge. The experience of the WCD provides a useful starting point for developing a plan of action. If the United Nations were to act in such an entrepreneurial fashion in issue areas critical to its core mission, such initiatives could expand the organization's political legitimacy in powerful states and could be the basis for leveraging new resources.

From a broader perspective, the United Nations needs to carefully evaluate how many of those tracks it wants to pursue at the same time. The current structure, skill mix, and resources of the organization may pose real limits. This will also be influenced by the functions the network is supposed to perform. Developing and disseminating knowledge are likely to require less time and fewer resources than negotiating and setting standards. Nevertheless, making a commitment to any network, new or old, without following through would send the wrong signal to clients and partners.

ROLES FOR THE UNITED NATIONS IN GPP NETWORKS

To make this ambitious but by no means unrealistic three-track approach work, the United Nations and its specialized agencies can play a number of roles in these networks: convenor, provider of a platform and "safe space," social entrepreneur, norm entrepreneur, multilevel-network manager, and capacity-builder. Prioritizing is therefore not just a matter of making a commitment to an existing network or supporting a new one. It also requires a clear under-standing of the specific role or roles the United Nations is prepared to perform in the network and the results that its involvement is expected to deliver. This needs to be communicated to the other network participants, so that partnerships do not falter because of false expectations. Indeed, transparent and reliable partnerships will be a critical success factor in executing all of the above functions. The United Nations should take greater advantage of the growing interest of other organizations in supporting GPP networks. On the private-sector side, the International Chamber of Commerce already cooperates with a number of UN agencies in the GPP agenda. Similarly, the World Economic Forum has demonstrated a growing interest in this topic. Its members, convening power, and the recently launched Center for the Global Agenda make it a valuable partner in network facilitation and management.

THE UNITED NATIONS AS CONVENOR

Some of the UN's most critical roles have been played behind the scenes, bringing key stakeholders together and creating the necessary conditions for consensual knowledge-building. It does this by brokering deals and mobilizing key constituencies for the effective operation of networks. Perhaps the organization's most consistent and unique contribution to the emergence and operation of GPP networks has been — and should be — in convening networks. UN agencies have demonstrated comparative advantage in organizing and convening meetings on issues where conflicts arise across the North–South divide. They have also shown comparative advantage in contributing to processes of consensual knowledge-building in a wide range of scientific and technical fields: examples include UNEP, WHO, and the technical agencies. UN agencies are often accepted more readily as intermediaries in developing countries than the Bretton Woods institutions because the UN agencies are not seen as being dominated by the industrial countries.

UNITED NATIONS AGENCIES AS PROVIDERS OF A PLATFORM AND A SAFE SPACE

UN agencies have provided a platform and a safe space for people and institutions coming together in a network. The agencies do this by providing a level playing field for negotiations and for consensual knowledge-building. UN agencies can thus be catalysts for networks, as was the United Nations Conference on Trade and Development (UNCTAD) with its Partners for Development summit meeting. That meeting served as a locus for information and knowledge exchange for partnership-building between UNCTAD and other state and non-state actors. Unlike most intergovernmental meetings, Partners for Development was not concerned with the negotiation of an agreed text. Instead, UNCTAD acted as a matchmaker, bringing together interested outside parties around established aspects of the organization's work. Another good example of catalytic engagement is the collaboration between the World Bank and the IUCN in the establishment of the WCD.

By acting as a platform, the United Nations can and should facilitate partnerships between NGOs and the business community. Collaborative links between these two constituencies are tentative and only just beginning, often against a backdrop of a long history of confrontation and conflict. The United Nations can help these two sectors identify the benefits of working together in trisectoral networks.

UNITED NATIONS STAFF AS SOCIAL ENTREPRENEURS

As discussed in Chapter 4, one of the clear lessons learned from the early stage of effective trisectoral networks is the importance of skilled entrepreneurial leadership. UN officials who have provided such leadership include James Grant of the United Nations Children's Fund (UNICEF) and Mustafa Tolba of UNEP, during negotiations of the CBD, the UNFCCC, and Agenda 21. Currently, Gro Harlem Brundtland at WHO, Carol Bellamy of UNICEF, and Klaus Töpfer of UNEP, among others, play such roles. But important as such high-profile leadership is in the initiation phase of a network, both UN agencies and staff should also focus their social entrepreneurship on such aspects as inclusion, effectiveness, and results once the network is operational. Thus, UN agencies and staff may play various roles at the same time in a network, or the same agency may play various roles in various phases of the policy cycle.

UNITED NATIONS AGENCIES AS NORM ENTREPRENEURS

UN agencies can also act as norm entrepreneurs or advocates by using networks as platforms to advance norms in such areas as sustainable human development, human rights, and disarmament. UNICEF in the 1980s, joined since 1990 by the UNDP, with its annual *Human Development Report*, has reshaped the analytical framework and the discourse on development issues. UNICEF has also done so with respect to landmines, child soldiers, and other children's-rights issues. UNHCHR is primarily a norm entrepreneur, and it has exercised such leadership through its de facto advocacy coalition with like-minded states and NGOs for the creation of the International Criminal Court. Recent secretaries-general have been important advocates for a range of disarmament issues, including landmine removal and the CWC.

UNITED NATIONS AGENCIES AS MULTILEVEL-NETWORK MANAGERS

The most challenging role of the United Nations with respect to networks, and an increasingly important one, is that of a multilevel-network manager. In the case of the RBM initiative, for example, WHO is involved in coordinating program activities, and the World Bank and WHO are involved in working with transnational and domestic health-sector-reform constituencies in developing countries to consolidate change coalitions. The organizations support these reform efforts by providing technical assistance and financial resources. For the learning dimension to work well, engagement at multiple levels is vital.

With the dual trends of greater devolution of authority through decentralization and the strengthening of supranational forms of governance, the challenge for the United Nations is to develop strategies for interacting with the appropriate levels of governance on particular issues at appropriate stages of the public-policy cycle. Once the local–global dimension of inclusion is being taken seriously and the network moves to implementation, the function of a multilevel-network manager will become very important, in conjunction with the function of capacity-building.

UNITED NATIONS AGENCIES AS CAPACITY-BUILDERS

As Chapter 4 has shown, capacity-building to enable more widespread participation in networks (input capacity) is key to ensuring inclusiveness, from both local–global and North–South perspectives. But capacity-building has a second dimension with respect to implementation, as discussed in Chapter 3. From that perspective, capacity-building is also critical to ensuring actual implementation and thus results (output capacity). The United Nations has a role to play in leveraging resources, both to enable people and organizations to participate in a network and to strengthen their ability to live up to their commitments.

As the examples in Chapter 4 have illustrated, capacity-building on the input side involves identifying and addressing gaps in financial, organizational, human, and knowledge resources that prevent organizations from working effectively in GPP networks. An important step in that direction is the UNDP's Sustainable Development Networking program. This partnership of governments, businesses, and NGOs is designed to help developing countries acquire the capacity to contribute solutions for sustainable development and to access solutions contributed by others, through the new ICTs. But more needs to be done.

In many cases, state and nonstate actors in developed and developing countries alike need to develop capacities to help monitor the policies that GPP networks have implemented — the GEF is an example where this has been done. Although industrial-country groups often also need to build capacity, the UN's focus should be on developing-country groups, simply for the sake of equity. Given that additional financial resources are unlikely to be forthcoming, one way to do this would be to strengthen current ties with networks that invest in sharing information, experiences, and resources, such as the Global Knowledge Partnership recently launched by the World Bank (Box 16).

Box 16
The Global Knowledge Partnership

~ The Global Knowledge Partnership (GKP) is an evolving informal partnership of more than 50 public institutions, businesses, and NGOs from industrial and developing countries;

~ It is committed to the idea that sharing information about experiences and resources is an effective way of ensuring equitable development;

~ Members of the GKP feel that the information revolution can be a positive force in providing individuals and communities with the resources they need to ensure sustainable development;

~ It takes shape from the idea that increased partnership and learning among the public, the business community, and not-for-profit organizations will ensure the inclusion of the poorest states and people of the world;

~ It has adopted a range of regional platforms that seek to improve access to knowledge and guarantee inclusion of all partners;

~ It organizes regional workshops and seminars to increase the exchange of knowledge in various communities and train citizens in the use of new technology;

~ It designs its various activities so as to produce such concrete results as improvements in agricultural practices, better employment opportunities, and improved access to telephones, computers, and other knowledge tools;

~ It admits as members those organizations that agree to support at least one initiative being conducted by the partnership; and

~ It is coordinated by the World Bank Institute with a small and informal secretariat.

Find out more about the GKP at **www.globalknowledge.org** on the Internet.

The United Nations has already demonstrated comparative advantage, relative to other international organizations in state capacity-building, through the UNDP's governance program and the UMP. State capacity remains critical for effective participation in, and implementation of, GPP networks. Indeed, implementation of many GPPs relies upon state capacity at the national and local levels. The participation of civil society and business is not a substitute for capable and effective state institutions but a complement to them. The combination of scarce resources and political constraints means that for the foreseeable future, the United Nations will and should emphasize the building of state capacity at the national and local levels while supporting other efforts to provide resources for building capacity in civil society. To the extent that activities directed to state capacity-building are undertaken with a network framework in place, such activities will generate their own demand for building the capacity of states to engage in trisectoral networks and the capacity of their partners (civil society and business) to participate in such networks.

THE UNITED NATIONS AS FINANCIER

Although it is an increasingly difficult role for the organization to play, the United Nations sometimes acts as a financier, providing resources for a range of operational programs related to the implementation of GPPs. Examples include immunization and reproductive health projects, projects to eliminate land mines, microfinance projects, and disease eradication and control projects. In some cases the United Nations serves as an intermediary, distributing earmarked funds supplied by others (for example, in the area of reproductive health); in others it contributes its own resources (as in microfinance); and in many others it does both (in landmine action and immunization).

It is crucial for the United Nations to facilitate the participation of disempowered or marginalized constituencies in ongoing networks or in networks that they help initiate. Thereby the United Nations can play the overall role of ensuring the inclusion of constituencies that are affected by the issue tackled by a particular network but are often left out of these policy processes, such as women or the poor and disenfranchised.

When taking over any of these roles, the United Nations has to know when to cut its losses and move to other venues with more promising opportunities. Political stalemates, after all, do not only occur outside the UN system. To minimize the waste of scarce resources, UN staff and member-country delegations need to identify when the "UN process" — the laborious process of consensus-building among large groups of states — only contributes to stalemate. Often this results from the ability of a small number of powerful states to effectively derail consensus. In such situations, staff should support efforts to move initiatives outside the system and redirect its support.

The landmines case illustrates perhaps most clearly how the UN process can become an obstacle to progress. The Ottawa process was begun by an alliance between some like-minded states and NGOs, reacting to a stalemate within the UN system. Some specialized agencies of the United Nations became active supporters. The forests case is one where increasing complexity — in the form of linkages between forest issues and other environmental, economic, and social issues — combined with intergovernmental stalemate virtually stifled progress. As the case study shows, there is little or no consensual knowledge that unites stakeholders in this issue area. In cases where the intergovernmental process has failed, such as in negotiations on the forest convention, NGOs have initiated their own networks. An example is the Forest Stewardship Council, where NGOs have joined with some actors from the business sector (governments were and are still excluded), with the overall aim of making progress on certification issues. The United Nations should focus its efforts on supporting and learning from such efforts.

In sum, despite the excitement that always comes from creating an open process and from pulling diverse sectors and resources together, the United Nations must approach networking soberly. It must consider in every instance whether there is sufficient interest and whether it has sufficient capacity and comparative advantage to play a productive and worthwhile role in the network. This presupposes a number of management changes within the UN system.

MAKING THE UNITED NATIONS FIT FOR GPP NETWORKS

MECHANISMS FOR ISSUE PRIORITIZATION AND COORDINATION

With a large number of initiatives launched just during the last few years, GPP networks are developing into a growth industry, increasing the need for a strategic approach. To become more selective in its network involvement and to better coordinate global network initiatives, the United Nations needs first to develop mechanisms for prioritizing and coordinating those nascent issues that call for UN involvement. It also needs to ensure that its own activities neither duplicate the work of other multilateral organizations nor work at cross-purposes to them.

TAKING STOCK

As a first step, the UN system should take stock of ongoing GPP initiatives in which it is involved. Such an overview would not only help to get a comprehensive perspective on the organization's activities but also likely detect potential room for synergies and better coordination among UN agencies. In addition, a UN-wide survey could take advantage of the vast pool of knowledge that already exists among the staff about network management and implementation. The survey should identify current institutional hurdles and bottlenecks and ask what concrete steps management can take to facilitate the UN's role as a network entrepreneur. Finally, strategic choice cannot be informed only by how important an initiative is; it must also consider how good an organization is at executing such an initiative. Therefore, an overview of this kind should also arrive at a preliminary cost–benefit analysis of individual initiatives and the UN's ultimate impact and how it can be improved. This requires external input from clients and partners addressing the UN's legitimacy, positioning, and strategic thrust, as well as the operational impact and measurable results of GPP networks on the ground.

ADDRESSING SELECTIVITY AND INTERAGENCY COORDINATION

UN participation in GPP networks has been at its most effective when several agencies have participated, each bringing its own comparative advantages to the process. For example, in the Polio Eradication Network, WHO provides the global technical leadership and overall coordination; UNICEF acts as the major provider of vaccines and immunization equipment and as the program's global advocate, also playing a key role in social mobilization and providing operational support in the field. In the RBM initiative, WHO provides technical assistance and coordination, and the World Bank provides policy advice on health-sector reform. Comparative advantages are most readily identified when stakeholders and policy objectives are explicit and the objectives are shared, rather than being obscured or contested. Interagency coordination is needed at the head-quarters level as well, as in on-the-ground implementation. The Administrative Committee on Coordination (ACC) and the United Nations Development Group (UNDG) are two venues within the UN system that could complement each other's activities to fulfill the many tasks that successful network management, including implementation, requires. The "issue-management system" would provide an ideal vehicle through which GPP networks could be established.

In principle, the ACC could offer a venue wherein priorities could be identified, and thereafter it could coordinate interagency collaboration with respect to the overall strategy. Obviously, the actual identification of priorities has to involve far-reaching external consultations conducted by agencies individually. But as far as prioritization within the United Nations is concerned, the ACC could ensure that the agencies' own strategic priorities are sufficiently taken into account. To ensure that networks do not work at cross-purposes with existing priorities, coordination, too, could rely on the ACC. Specifically, the Secretary-General's reform agenda (as laid out in his report "Renewing the United Nations: A Programme for Reform") recognizes that

> Traditional processes of coordination need to be supplemented by a series of practical arrangements which provide for more active, cooperative management ... both within the United Nations system and extending to other involved intergovernmental and non-governmental organizations.

Arrangements of this kind are not entirely new. Examples include the working groups and task forces that have emerged over the past decade as mechanisms for preparing for, and following up on, the series of global conferences held in the 1990s.

This need for more informal processes coincides with a slight shift in the ACC's agenda. As a result of ongoing strategic discussions and coordination activities, the ACC has become engaged in substantive discussions on issues facing the world community. These issues cannot be addressed by a single UN agency with a mandate to lead, and they have pushed the ACC beyond its narrow role of administrative coordination toward acting as a deliberative body that releases the outcomes of discussions aimed at having an impact on governments, civil society, and business. To further facilitate selectivity and coordination at the global level, as well as create more space for the ACC's emerging policy role, the Secretary-General's reform program provided for the establishment of an issue-management system, which could serve as the foundation for GPP networks. The concept of an issue-management system, which is now in the early stage of implementation through the Secretariat of the ACC, is not without precedent. It had its origins in the initiative undertaken by the Secretariat of the United Nations Conference on Environment and Development (UNCED) in developing Agenda 21. Issue-specific working parties or task forces would be composed of a representative from each of the principal organizations with an interest or capacity in the area concerned and would be headed by a lead organization that would also provide secretariat support. The working party or task force could be established either for an indefinite period (for issues demanding ongoing cooperation) or on an ad hoc, time-limited basis (to respond to short-term needs for cooperation).

The growing deliberative policy role of the ACC has the potential to overcome the current fragmentation in addressing the growing complexity of many global challenges. Moreover, a more flexible organizational approach could enhance UN participation in GPP networks in three ways. First, it would enable the United Nations to respond more rapidly to GPP issues. Second, it could help the organization deploy its limited human resources in a more targeted and effective manner. Third, it would address the recurring complaints from states, NGOs, the business sector, and other international organizations that UN interagency coordination is weak.

Take sustainable development for example. The principal UN organization dealing with the environment is UNEP, whose policy directions are given by its governing council. The recently formed Department of Economic and Social Affairs, which services the Commission on Sustainable Development, has a major respon-sibility for sustainable development and the follow-up to the Rio Conference. At the intersecretariat level, the main mechanism for coordination is provided by the Inter-Agency Committee on Sustainable Development (IACSD) of the ACC, which, despite early problems, is functioning fairly well through its system of task managers and assigns "lead" coordinating roles to its members, depending upon the sectoral issues being dealt with in the context of Agenda 21. In addition, UNEP also has an Environment Coordination Group. Both the Economic and Social Council

(ECOSOC) and the Second Committee of the General Assembly
also continue to play an important policy and coordination role
in the environmental and sustainable development areas.

To bring more clarity to the current proliferation of forums where
environment and sustainable development issues are discussed or
coordinated, at both the intergovernmental and the interagency
levels, the IACSD could develop general policy directions in the area
of sustainable development, and the ACC Task Force could set basic
guidelines for interagency cooperation; the role of UNEP would be
to develop environmental policies and facilitate arrangements with
UN institutions for their coordinated implementation. This is, in
fact, the general direction toward which the UN system has been
moving since 1992. This division of labour would enable network
partners to engage in discussions or activities at the appropriate
levels; at the same time, it would maximize the UN's impact in global
policy networks organized around sustainable development issues.

As discussed above, developing both input and output capacities is
critical for the success of any network. Thus, not only the UN's
mission but also its role in network facilitation suggests strong support for network capacity-building. The coordination of activities
at the national and local levels has traditionally been a weak
spot of operational and field-related activities. As an umbrella
organization, the UNDG is, in principle, well positioned to serve
as a coordinator for network capacity-building, by facilitating a
process that enables network partners in the United Nations to
prioritize capacity-building according to need and comparative
advantage.

This role aligns squarely with the UNDG's central goal of strengthening the policy and program coherence and the effectiveness of UN
development activities. The coordination of capacity-building
efforts would be an integral step in establishing a UN Development
Assistance Framework. It could build on the efforts to harmonize
the program cycles for individual countries and develop into a
cross-country effort to enhance the UN's efforts in capacity-building
operations. By acting as a backstop for GPP networks, especially as
far as capacity-building and implementation are concerned, the

UNDG could provide a suitable complement to the network-related activities of the ACC, establishing an integrated framework for network prioritization and coordination in the UN system.

COORDINATING A MULTILATERAL DIVISION OF LABOUR

A comprehensive strategy for network prioritization and coordination must reach far beyond the UN system. The United Nations should engage its counterparts — the World Bank, the World Trade Organization, the IMF, the regional development institutions, and, where appropriate, collective security institutions — in a dialogue on selectivity and prioritization. The aim of this dialogue should be to achieve a division of labour that identifies lead institutions, to be supported by others with relevant expertise. Some central but "light" coordination may be helpful (see below), but actual operations should be coordinated through informal task forces that represent the interested institutions and are empowered to operate with the fewest possible layers of bureaucracy in the various multilateral institutions. Given the changing nature of the international system, international organizations will face a growing demand for global risk management and crisis response from member governments and other constituents. Anything but a highly agile and informal global response team with full support from its parent institutions is unlikely to be able to meet that demand.

SUPPORTING THE UNITED NATIONS SYSTEM

The United Nations should support the establishment of a clearing-house for GPP networks. This clearinghouse, provided with a small secretariat, could act as a hub for network-related activities both within the United Nations and beyond. As a centre for knowledge management, the clearinghouse would

⤳ Ensure that interested parties are informed about ongoing network activities both inside and outside the United Nations;

⤳ Identify potential areas for new network activity; and

⤳ Disseminate knowledge and lessons about best practices.

Creating a website and publishing a newsletter would make the centre accessible to a broad audience, including those who play a principal role in providing relevant information.

Such a clearinghouse could also build internal capacity by supporting programs to provide UN staff with training periods in civil
society, business, and governments. Sabbaticals and secondments
would allow these staff members to work in the private or the
nonprofit sector to gain first-hand knowledge of how that sector
works. Whether such a clearinghouse is best located within the UN
system or outside it is an issue that deserves careful consideration.

REACHING OUT TO EXTERNAL PARTNERS

For the United Nations to become an active player in GPP networks,
it needs to reach out to its external partners. Coalition-building
involves identifying unmobilized constituencies and strengthening
existing ones to move forward on the implementation of existing
networks. To evolve into a credible intermediary between sectors,
the United Nations has to strengthen its efforts to enter into a
fruitful and cooperative dialogue with NGOs and the business
community.

In recent years, the United Nations has missed opportunities for
strengthening relations with NGOs. In 1995, the Commission on
Global Governance put on the record that "UN–NGO relationships
are improving." As Ed Luck pointed out in a recent report to the
Commission, the same cannot be said a mere 5 years later. The
United Nations has failed to take advantage of the dramatic increase
in civil society's interest in participation, which was the legacy of the
significant expansion of NGO participation in the series of world
conferences. These gains are now threatened by a reduction in
NGOs' access to the meetings set up to evaluate progress toward the
commitments made at those conferences. They are also threatened
by the glacial pace with which new mechanisms are being created for
NGOs to interact with the new organizational processes that resulted
from those conferences, such as the IACSD. These weak or worsening
relations do not bode well for the UN's bid to pursue any of the
three tracks proposed above.

The institution's interaction with nonprofit foundations could also
be strengthened. UN agencies are involved in some networks that
include nonprofit foundations: WHO is involved in networks
dedicated to disease eradication; FAO and UNDP worked closely with

the Ford and Rockefeller foundations in creating CGIAR. Although the foundations have become a less important factor in CGIAR, the working relationship continues to this day. But in general, the United Nations has not developed strong relationships with foundations. Such relationships will be particularly important if the organization hopes to leverage funds in a period of scarce financial resources. The United Nations Foundation might be tasked to serve as a coordinator between the United Nations and other foundations. The Secretary-General's report on the UN system's interactions with NGOs identifies areas where insufficient financial resources hinder greater cooperation between them, as well as some areas where member countries could assist the United Nations in facilitating such cooperation. Follow-up by the Secretariat or another entity, such as the proposed clearinghouse, to encourage member-country delegations to facilitate such cooperation is required.

NGOs have offered a range of proposals to strengthen the various formal mechanisms for enhancing their participation in UN activities, to strengthen UN–NGO partnerships, to increase resources for the Non-Governmental Liaison Service (NGLS), and to revive the trust fund for developing-country NGOs to provide funding for travel and other costs associated with participation at UN events and meetings. As many of our case studies have shown, this is a critical issue if inclusion of local and developing-country actors is to work. This report endorses these proposals, as they should promote the UN's credibility and legitimacy as a facilitator of networks. The United Nations should also work with the developing-country-led International Forum on Capacity Building to create a privately administered, voluntary fund to support capacity-building activities for NGOs in developing countries.

The United Nations has yet to develop a system-wide, formal mechanism for interacting with the business community, apart from business associations accredited as NGOs. Corporations are powerful and important stakeholders whose participation is critical to the success of many networks. NGOs have various formal mechanisms for interaction with the United Nations, including consultative status with ECOSOC, accreditation with the Department of Public Information, and the NGLS. The UN technical agencies have regular contact with businesses, and some of the development and humanitarian agencies have operational interactions with them, but there is no system-wide strategic framework along those lines. The private sector should be offered similar access. One possible institutional mechanism for private-sector–United Nations interaction would be an interagency liaison service for the private sector.

The Global Compact — an initiative launched by the UN Secretary-General in his 1999 speech at the World Economic Forum — can be seen as a first and important step toward a more systematic relationship between the United Nations and the for-profit private sector. The Compact correctly assumes that the challenge of closing the governance gaps has to be met at the microlevel, by involving individual companies. It also realizes the importance of addressing collective-action problems on the business side, by promoting cooperation with business associations.

However, for the United Nations to play a greater role in global norm- and standards-setting, a trisectoral approach is key. As we have seen in several of the cases reviewed for this report, such as the WCD and the MAI, the legitimacy and effectiveness of global norm- and standards-setting initiatives depend on the participation of all stakeholders. Participants need to be selected with great care, respecting such principles as balance of power and inclusiveness. Thus, in addition to each individual effort, the United Nations faces the challenge of linking its initiatives with NGOs and businesses. This is certainly a demanding task, but if it engages with NGOs and the business sector separately, rather than acting as a convenor for all sectors, the United Nations risks undermining both its credibility and its effectiveness. This is echoed in the concerns and criticisms raised in conjunction with the organization's recent initiatives toward closer cooperation with the business sector. Some NGOs and even some member governments claim that these initiatives allow companies to exploit the United Nations for a cheap public-relations advantage and even enable corporations to set the policy agendas of the UN agencies involved, to which they provide much-needed financial resources.

A trisectoral approach would address these concerns by facilitating collaboration between civil society and the business sector. One stepping-stone to improving relations and entering into a constructive strategic dialogue with key actors from the business and NGO communities would be to develop the Global Compact on a trisectoral basis. By making itself a safe place for all the key actors to convene to negotiate politically controversial issues, the United Nations could fill a major gap in governance.

The ultimate currency of GPP networks is their ability to effectively marry knowledge with power. In today's world, the United Nations needs to pay attention to its ability to offer itself as a safe place, not only for its traditional stakeholders — member governments — but also for the business community and civil society. Trisectoral networks provide a mechanism for the United Nations to rebuild its credibility and, indeed, the only way to achieve its increasingly complex missions with scarce resources in the 21st century. The organization's ability to effectively initiate, maintain, and participate in such networks will largely determine the extent to which it can achieve its mission — not least in the eyes of its constituents.

By successfully engaging in GPP networks, the United Nations performs a vital service to its member states. It is they that are ultimately strengthened by these networks' activities. Networks help member states take advantage of the benefits and address the challenges of technological change and economic and social integration and thus perform their duties to their citizens in a more effective and legitimate way.

Chapter 6

CONCLUSION

The United Nations is at a critical juncture. In an increasingly interconnected world, new forms of global governance have emerged. GPP networks embrace the very forces of globalization that have confounded and complicated traditional governance structures, challenging the operational capacity and democratic responsiveness of governments. They are distinctive in their ability to bring people and institutions from diverse backgrounds together, often when they have been working against one another for years. Making use of the strength of weak ties, networks can handle this diversity of actors precisely because of the productive tensions on which they rest. As UN Secretary-General Kofi Annan has stated, "This partnership of NGOs, the private sector, international organizations and governments ... is a powerful partnership for the future." GPP networks thus represent a promising medium through which the United Nations can achieve its mission, maintain its relevance in a changing global environment, and serve its members in a more effective and efficient way.

But they also represent a unique opportunity for governments to regain the initiative in the debate over the future of global governance. It is crucial for member states of the United Nations to understand that GPP networks are meant not to replace governments but to complement them. Empowering those entities that constitute the real basis of legitimate and accountable global governance amounts to neither a zero-sum game nor a power shift. Rather, it provides an opportunity to strengthen those institutions that are charged with the execution of policy. Networks enable governments to better manage the risks and take advantage of the opportunities that economic liberalization and technological change bring, making governments more responsive to their constituents.

This report has barely skimmed the surface in its survey of the processes and dynamics of trisectoral networks. A comparative examination of recent experiences suggests that networks perform a number of functions. By bringing together actors from different

sectors to address specific transnational issues, networks place those
issues on the global governance agenda and pressure existing structures to take action. Networks also convene multiple stakeholders
in setting regulations and designing standards, and they are deeply
involved in the development and dissemination of knowledge. Some
networks seek to create markets where they do not yet exist and to
deepen them where they are falling short of their potential. Several
global networks have been formed to assist in the implementation of
intergovernmental treaties. And by involving actors from multiple
sectors and levels in the policy-making process, all networks work
toward closing the participatory gap in global governance.

However, for GPP networks to become a reliable and more widely
used instrument in the arsenal of global governance, the United
Nations has to become an active player. It has to help address the
managerial challenges and current weaknesses in these networks,
most of all the dual challenge of inclusion. Whether networks
become legitimate governance structures and can implement policies on the ground will ultimately depend upon greater inclusion of
participants from developing countries and from local institutions
at all stages of the policy cycle.

Two roles for the United Nations in particular stand out. The
first is derived from the need for greater inclusiveness in global
decision-making. The United Nations should be charged with
creating an enabling environment that permits countries, especially
in the developing world, to participate in the establishment of
trisectoral networks and enables them to implement and enforce the
decisions made in these networks in their own domestic institutional
and policy context. This includes a focus on capacity-building,
widespread dissemination of information, and establishment of a
knowledge base that empowers all parties involved to contribute to
the debate over the public-policy issue at hand.

The second role stems from the fact that international organizations
in general and the United Nations in particular are in a good
position to provide a platform for convening trisectoral networks.
Taking on the roles of enabler of existing networks and convenor
of new ones presupposes a greater humility, some internal capacity-
building on the part of international organizations to ensure a

greater emphasis on selectivity, and coordination among them to minimize competition. In reality, however, international organizations often still prefer a bureaucratic, top-down approach that threatens to suffocate the dynamism of emerging networks. For this reason it might be best for now to position networks outside those organizations, to avoid burdening them with the existing organizations' still unresolved internal problems.

To become reliable team players in GPP networks, the United Nations and its specialized agencies have to implement a number of organizational changes, including mechanisms for prioritizing and coordinating nascent issues. Although GPP networks offer an innovative and dynamic approach to governance, they will not work without adjustments to all their component parts. Collaboration in networks for global public-policy-making requires adjustment on the part of both network participants and the existing institutions in charge of public policy, that is, states and international organizations. This raises a number of critical issues with regard to institutional management, learning, and change, which were discussed in more detail in Chapter 4 and, specifically with regard to the United Nations, in Chapter 5.

Equally important, governments should not divert funding from other important fields to meet the needs of networks. Rather, they should see participation in trisectoral networks as long-term investments that will ultimately help them meet their responsibilities. In particular, resources spent on ensuring broad inclusiveness in GPP networks that protect the global environment, that fight and contain the spread of communicable diseases, that battle transnational crime, and that ensure food security in today's world are neither "foreign" nor "aid." Rather, they are a global public investment that generates a real return, and one that is shared by all. Governments remain the primary actors, responsible for a wide range of activities, particularly development programs. As UNICEF Executive Director Carol Bellamy has said, "We must not let governments off the hook." GPP networks must therefore be seen as complements to national and intergovernmental governance structures, and not as substitutes.

Civil society and the private sector must also adjust to better participate in trisectoral networks. Greater transparency, in particular, is
necessary. Principles of disclosure-based regulation, guaranteeing
other groups sufficient access to ensure that their interests are
adequately represented, would build confidence in such a structure.
Corporations can also facilitate networks by improving their own
internal control and management structures, to encourage dialogue
with other sectors. Independent audits and incentive structures
that discourage excessive risk-taking are examples of measures that
are readily available. The greater the focus on better corporate
governance, the lower the risk of market failure and the need
for outside regulation. A growing number of corporations and
business associations have begun to take the lead in implementing
this agenda for change and have become pioneers in GPP. For their
part, a number of NGOs have also realized the need for greater
transparency and accountability.

As was hinted in the introduction, we may well be in the early
stages of a paradigm shift (in Thomas Kuhn's sense) in the area of
governance. The frontiers of knowledge still need to be explored,
and ultimately, practice will inform our theorizing. At this stage,
however, the prime task is to assemble the lessons learned from
existing networks so as to explore the challenges on the way ahead.
A clearinghouse could help with this by serving as a hub, a centre
for knowledge management that assembles and disseminates the
lessons learned in networks around the world.

In sum, GPP networks do not offer an easy ride, but the difficulties
are well worth the risk, given the daunting challenges of a complex
world with an ever-expanding multiplicity of actors, interests, and
issues to be resolved. Many new and competing interests have sur-
faced since the end of the Cold War, and where they come into
conflict, those conflicts need to be mediated. For too long, the
centre of the debate has been left vacant, the podium having
been abandoned to the extremes on both ends of the ideological
spectrum. It is time to think about how the middle ground can be
regained by engaging the different parties in a dialogue — a dialogue
that would help to reoccupy the centre and initiate a process of

searching for sustainable responses to the challenges of globalization.

The stakes are high. Globalization is not, after all, the end of history. It is time to take a proactive stance lest we witness a full-fledged backlash against globalization. The status quo is unsustainable, and a change for the worse by forcing globalization back into national boundaries — "moving forward into the past" — is not an unlikely scenario. Networks can help to change this unsustainable status quo for the better by responding to the challenges and taking full advantage of technological change and economic and social integration. Mindful of these benefits, governments are throwing more weight behind GPP networks. Ultimately, it is up to the political will of the member states to fully endorse such a course. But it is the duty of the United Nations to lay out to its members the challenges that face them at the dawning of a new millennium and provide them with an achievable agenda for meeting those challenges.

ACRONYMS AND ABBREVIATIONS

ACC	Administrative Committee on Coordination [UN]
AIP	Apparel Industry Partnership
CBD	Convention on Biological Diversity
CFCs	chlorofluorocarbons
CGIAR	Consultative Group on International Agricultural Research
CWC	Chemical Weapons Convention
ECOSOC	Economic and Social Council [UN]
FAO	Food and Agricultural Organization of the United Nations
FDI	foreign direct investment
FLA	Fair Labor Association
GAVI	Global Alliance for Vaccines and Immunization
GEF	Global Environment Facility
GFAR	Global Forum on Agricultural Research
GKP	Global Knowledge Partnership
GPP	global public policy
GWP	Global Water Partnership
IACSD	Inter-Agency Committee on Sustainable Development
ICBL	International Campaign to Ban Landmines
ICTs	information and communication technologies
IDRC	International Development Research Centre
IFF	Intergovernmental Forum on Forests
IFI	international financial institution
ILO	International Labour Organization [UN]
IMF	International Monetary Fund
IPF	Intergovernmental Panel on Forests

ISAB	International Scientific Advisory Board
ISO	International Standardization Organization
IUCN	World Conservation Union (International Union for the Conservation of Nature and Natural Resources)
MAI	Multilateral Agreement on Investment
MLF	Multilateral Fund
MMV	Medicines for Malaria Venture
NGLS	Non-Governmental Liaison Service [UN]
NGO	nongovernmental organization
OECD	Organisation for Economic Co-operation and Development
RBM	Roll Back Malaria initiative
TI	Transparency International
UMP	Urban Management Programme
UNCED	United Nations Conference on Environment and Development
UNCHS	United Nations Centre for Human Settlements
UNCTAD	United Nations Conference on Trade and Development
UNDG	United Nations Development Group
UNDP	United Nations Development Programme
UNEP	United Nations Environment Programme
UNFCCC	United Nations Framework Convention on Climate Change
UNHCHR	Office of the United Nations High Commissioner for Human Rights
UNICEF	United Nations Children's Fund
WCD	World Commission on Dams
WHO	World Health Organization

CASE STUDIES OF THE UN VISION PROJECT ON GLOBAL PUBLIC POLICY NETWORKS

SIMON BAGSHAW
Promoting Implementation of
the Guiding Principles of
Internal Displacement

DAVID BOBROWSKY
Creating a Global Public Policy
Network in the Apparel
Industry: The Apparel Industry
Partnership

ELIZABETH DONNELLY
Proclaiming the Jubilee: The
Debt and Structural Adjustment
Network

CURTIS FARRAR
A Case Study of the Consultative
Group on International
Agricultural Research

FREDRIK GALTUNG
A Global Public Policy Network
to Curb Corruption: The
Experience of Transparency
International

REINER GRUNDMANN
The Protection of the Ozone
Layer

ASTRID HARNISCH
Managing our Forests:
The Intergovernmental
Panel on Forests and the
Intergovernmental Forum on
Forests (IPF/IFF) Processes

VIRGINIA HAUFLER
Negotiating Standards for
Environmental Management
Systems: ISO 14000

PAUL HOHNEN
Greenpeace and the Financial
Sector: The Possibility of
Profitable Relationships
Between Not-for-profits and
For-profits.

SANJEEV KHAGRAM
Beyond Temples and Tombs:
Towards Effective Governance
for Sustainable Development
Through the World Commission
on Dams

STUART MASLEN
Lessons Learned from the
International Campaign to End
the Use of Children as Soldiers

Anna Ohanyan
The Politics of Microcredit

Oluwemimo Oluwasola
The City Consultation Method
of Urban Management
Programme (UMP) as a Policy
Strategy to Fight Urban Poverty

Ann Peters
International Partnerships on
the Road to Ban Anti-personnel
Landmines

Timothy Sisk
Global Networks for Democracy
Promotion Enhancing Local
Governance

Charlotte Streck
The Network Structure of the
Global Environment Facility

Katia Tieleman
The Failure of the Multilateral
Agreement on Investment (MAI)

Emmanuelle Tuerlings and
Julian Robinson
The Trilateral Network
Associated with the Chemical
Weapons Convention

Arjen van Ballegoyen
Roll Back Malaria: A WHO
Initiated Network in the Fight
Against Malaria

Lynn Wagner
The Sustainable Development
Imperative and the Travel and
Tourism Industry

I. William Zartman
Global Regime Evolution:
CSSDC in Africa

Workshop Participants

Throughout our project, we greatly profited from the discussions in the various workshops on global public-policy (GPP) networks. Workshops were held on 10 and 22 September and 8 November 1999. The first focused on the importance of trisectoral involvement and the roles of international organizations; the second, on the value and roles of international institutions and the skills needed to address global issues; and the third, on networking and discussion among the GPP practitioners at the workshop of their common themes and challenges, along with their views on regional and global public-policy networks and the constraints, weaknesses, and best practices for such networks.

10 SEPTEMBER WORKSHOP

DE JONGE OUDRAAT, CHANTAL
Carnegie Endowment for
International Peace

FARRAR, CURTIS
International Food Policy
Research Institute

FLORINI, ANN
Carnegie Endowment
for International Peace

HARNISCH, ASTRID
University of Potsdam

HAUFLER, VIRGINIA
Department of Government
and Politics, University of
Maryland

HOHNEN, PAUL
Greenpeace International

KANE, MICHAEL
Environmental Protection
Agency [United States]

KHAGRAM, SANJEEV
Kennedy School
of Government,
Harvard University

LYMAN, PRINCETON
Overseas Development Council

MÜRLE, HOLGER
Kennedy School of
Government, Harvard
University

OHANYAN, ANNA
Syracuse University

PETERS, ANN
Open Society Institute,
Washington

PICCIOTTO, ROBERT
The World Bank

RAO GUPTA, GEETA
International Center for
Research on Women

SAYED, ARSHAD
The World Bank, Corporate
Strategy Group

SIMMONS, P.J.
Carnegie Endowment for
International Peace

VAN BALLEGOYEN, ARJEN
School of Advanced
International Studies,
Johns Hopkins University

WASHINGTON, JOE
School of Human Rights
Research, Netherlands Institute
of Human Rights

WHITAKER, BETH
The Brookings Institution,
UN Vision Project on Global
Public Policy Networks

WITTE, JAN MARTIN
UN Vision Project on Global
Public Policy Networks

22 SEPTEMBER WORKSHOP (UNDP–WORLD BANK)

AGERSKOV, ANDERS
The World Bank, Strategy and
Resource Management

ASENJO, RAFAEL
United Nations Development
Programme, Global
Environment Facility

BARNES, SUZANNE
The World Bank,
Environmentally and Socially
Sustainable Development

BATSON, AMIE
The World Bank, Health,
Nutrition and Population

BETCHERMAN, GORDON
The World Bank, Social
Protection Team

BRISCOE, JOHN
The World Bank,
Global Water Unit

CHASE, BOB
World Learning

FARRAR, CURTIS
International Food Policy
Research Institute

FERRONI, MARCO
The World Bank, Resource
Mobilization and Cofinancing

GEER, SHIRLEY
The World Bank, Consultative
Group on International
Agricultural Research

GHANI, ASHRAF
The World Bank, Social
Development Department

HUBBARD, JOAN
The World Bank,
The World Bank Institute

HUBBARD, PAUL
The World Bank, Trust Funds
and Cofinancing Department

JOHNSON, IAN
The World Bank,
Environmentally and Socially
Sustainable Development

KARLSSON, MATS
The World Bank,
External Affairs

KARP, PHIL
The World Bank, Global
Knowledge Partnership

KAUL, INGE
United Nations Development
Programme, Office of
Development Studies

KEKEH, NICOLE
The World Bank,
External Affairs

KING, KENNETH
Global Environment Facility

KUSAKABE, MOTOO
The World Bank, Resource
Mobilization and Cofinancing

LEITERITZ, RALPH
The World Bank, Strategy and
Resource Management

LENTON, ROBERTO
United Nations Development
Programme, Sustainable Energy
and Environment Division

LEONE, GAETANO
United Nations Centre for
Human Settlements, The World
Bank, Transport, Water and
Urban Development

LIOUNIS, AUDREY
The World Bank,
External Affairs

LUINSTRA, AMY
The World Bank, Human
Development Network

MCPHAIL, KATHRYN
The World Bank, Social
Development Department

MOGENSEN, MICHAEL
The World Bank, Human
Development Network

NEERGAARD, FRODE
The World Bank, Nordic–Baltic
Executive-Director's Office

PARMAR, VIJAY
United Nations Development
Programme, IT/BDP

PICCIOTTO, ROBERT
The World Bank, Operations
Evaluation

SAXENIAN, HELEN
The World Bank, Health,
Nutrition and Population

SAYED, ARSHAD
The World Bank, Strategy and
Resource Management

SJOBERG, GEIR
United Nations Development
Programme, Energy and
Atmosphere Programme

SOOD, ANIL
The World Bank, Strategy and
Resource Management

STAHMER, ANNA
The World Bank,
World Bank Institute

STERN, MARC
United Nations Development
Programme, Office of
Development Studies

STONE, PAULA
The World Bank, Strategy and
Resource Management

STRECK, CHARLOTTE
UN Vision Project on Global
Public Policy Networks

TAMESIS, PAULINE
United Nations Development
Programme, MGDG

VIDAEUS, LARS
The World Bank, Environment
Department

WALKER, DIANA
The World Bank, Human
Development Network

WATANABE, EIMI
United Nations Development
Programme, Bureau for
Development Policy

WILKINS, JILL
The World Bank,
External Affairs

ZHENG, KANGBIN
The World Bank,
Partnerships Group

ZIEGLER, TOR
The World Bank,
Global Water Unit

ZULFIQAR, ARIF
The World Bank, Trust Funds
and Cofinancing Department

8 NOVEMBER WORKSHOP

ADU, KOFI
Ghana Association of Private
Voluntary Organizations in
Development

AGARWAL, ANIL
Centre for Science and
Environment India

AGERSKOV, ANDERS
The World Bank, Corporate
Strategy Group

AGYEYOMAH, COLEMAN
Small Business Development,
Community Water and
Sanitation Program Ghana

AKINYELE, ISAAC LAOLU
Society for International
Development, Department of
Human Nutrition, University
of Ibadan, Nigeria

ARAUCO LEMAITRE, LEONOR
UNITAS Bolivia

BERENBEIM, RONALD
Conference Board

BISELL, RICHARD
National Research Council
[United States]

BOSIRE, ERIC
Forestry Action Network
Nairobi

BUTTKEREIT, SÖREN
UN Vision Project on Global
Public Policy Networks

CAYOSA, EGON DOMINGO
NGOs for Integrated Protected
Areas Inc. – Philippines

CHAPARRO, ELKYN
The World Bank,
External Affairs

COSGROVE, WILLIAM J.
United Nations Educational,
Scientific and Cultural
Organization, Water Vision
Unit, World Water Council,
Division of Water Sciences

COURT, ROBERT
Rio Tinto

CREIGHTON, TRAVIS
UN Vision Project on Global
Public Policy Networks

CROSBY, ANDREW
International Centre for Trade
and Sustainable Development
Geneva

CUSIMANO, MARYANN
Catholic University of America

DETTKE, DIETER
Friedrich Ebert Foundation

DOS SANTOS, CARLOS
Ambassador of Mozambique
to the United Nations

FARRAR, CURTIS
International Food Policy
Research Institute

FERRONI, MARCO
The World Bank, Resource
Mobilization and Cofinancing

FLORINI, ANN
Carnegie Endowment for
International Peace

FRENCH, HILLARY
World Resources Institute

GITONA, ANASTASSIA
European Commission

GOLDBLATT, LAUREN
Pricewaterhouse Cooper LLP

GREENE, GEORGE
Green-World Consulting,
Ottawa

GROWN, CAREN
MacArthur Foundation

GRUENBERGER, JENNY
Foro Boliviano Medio Ambiente
y Desarrollo [Bolivian fund for
environmental protection and
development]

GRUNDMANN, REINER
Aston Business School

GUPTA, GEETA RAO
International Center for
Research on Women

GWIN, CATHERINE
The World Bank

HARNISCH, ASTRID
University of Potsdam

HAUFLER, VIRGINIA
University of Maryland,
Department of Government
and Politics

HIGGOTT, RICHARD
University of Warwick

HOHNEN, PAUL
Greenpeace International

HOLZ, HANS
ABB Group

ISENMAN, PAUL
United Nations Foundation

KAMPMANN, MARTINA
Gesellschaft für Technische
Zusammenarbeit [agency for
technical cooperation]

KANE, ANGELA
The United Nations

KANE, MICHAEL
Environmental Protection
Agency [United States]

KARLSSON, MATS
The World Bank, External
and UN Affairs

KAUL, INGE
United Nations Development
Programme, Office of
Development Studies

KEKEH, NICOLE
The World Bank, Strategy and
Campaign Group External
Affairs

KHAGRAM, SANJEEV
Kennedy School of
Government, Harvard
University

KICKBUSCH, ILONA
School of Medicine,
Yale University

KUCHENMÜLLER, REINHARD
Visuelle Protokolle

KUSAKABE, MOTOO
The World Bank, Resource
Mobilization and Cofinancing

LEE, BERNICE
The United Nations

LEITERITZ, RALF
The World Bank, Corporate
Strategy Group

MACK, ANDY
The United Nations

MASSIE, ROBERT KINLOCH
Global Reporting Initiative

McFARLANE, IAN
United Nations Development
Group Office

McGOFF, CHRIS
Group Decision Support
Systems Inc.

McPHAIL, KATHRYN
The World Bank

MERRILL, DOUGLAS
Center for Applied Policy
Research

MUELLER, MILTON
Syracuse University

MUELLER-KRAENNER, SASCHA
Heinrich Boell Foundation

O'CONNOR, LAURA
The World Bank, Corporate
Strategy Group

OHANYAN, ANNA
Syracuse University

OUDRAAT, CHANTAL DE JONGE
Carnegie Endowment for
International Peace

PENNA, FRANK
Policy Sciences Center Inc.

PETERS, ANN
Open Society Institute
Landmines Project

PINZLER, PETRA
Die Zeit

RECHY MONTIEL, MARIO
Center for Strategic Studies
Mexico

RENDER, JO
CIVICUS World Alliance for
Citizen Participation

RUSSELL, PETER EDWARD
The Chase Manhattan
Corporation

SAYED, ARSHAD
The World Bank, Corporate
Strategy Group

SCHOLZ, KATJA
The World Bank, Corporate
Strategy Group

SEITER, ANDREAS
Novartis

SENSER, ROBERT
Human Rights for Workers

SEYMOUR, FRANCES
World Resources Institute

SOUDRIETTE, RICHARD
International Foundation for
Election Systems

STRECK, CHARLOTTE
Humboldt University, Berlin

SY, MARIAM BABA
Association pour la lutte contre
les pratiques néfastes à la santé
de la mère et de l'enfant

TIELEMAN, KATIA
European University Institute,
Harvard University

TODD, JOHN
The World Bank, Corporate
Strategy Group

TUERLINGS, EMMANUELLE
Science and Technology Policy
Research, University of Sussex

VARUGHESE, GEORGE C.
Development Alternatives

VOGL, FRANK
Transparency International

WADDELL, STEVE
Organizational Futures Inc.

WILSON, KAREN
World Economic Forum

YACH, DEREK
World Health Organization

ZARTMAN, WILLIAM
School of Advanced
International Studies,
Johns Hopkins University

Bibliography

NETWORK THEORY, COLLABORATION, AND PARTNERSHIP

Börzel, T. 1998. Organizing Babylon: on the different conceptions of policy networks. Public Administration, 76.

Granovetter, M. 1973. The strength of weak ties. American Journal of Sociology, 6.

Messner, D. 1997. The network society: economic development and international competitiveness as problems of social governance. Frank Cass, London, UK.

Obser, A. 1999. Communicative structuration and governance of the global environment through policy networks of international aid organizations. Nomos, Baden-Baden, Germany.

Prewitt, K. 1998. Networks in international capacity-building: cases from Sub-Saharan Africa. Social Science Research Council, New York, NY, USA.

Rhodes, R.A.W.; Marsh, D. 1992. New directions in the study of policy networks. European Journal of Political Research, 21.

Thatcher, M. 1998. The development of policy network analyses: from modest origins to overarching frameworks. Journal of Theoretical Politics, 10.

Waddell, S. 1998. Tri-sectoral coproducers: a new type of development organization. Institute for Development Research, Boston, MA, USA.

———— 1999. Business–government–nonprofit collaborations as agents for social innovation and learning. Organizational Futures, Boston, MA, USA.

Waddell, S.; Brown, L.D. 1997. Fostering intersectoral partnering: a guide to promoting cooperation among governments, business, and civil society actors. IDRC Reports, 13(3).

Waddock, S. 1989. Understanding social partnerships: an evolutionary model of partnership organizations. Administration & Society, 21.

INTERNATIONAL ORGANIZATIONS, CHANGE, AND LEARNING

Ansell, C.K.; Weber, S. 1999. Organizing international politics: sovereignty and open systems. International Political Science Review, 20.

Barnett, M.N.; Finnemore, M. In press. The politics, power, and pathologies of international organizations. International Organization.

Cusimano, M.K. 1999. The challenge to institutions. *In* Beyond sovereignty: issues for a global agenda. Bedford/St Martin's, Boston, MA, USA.

Gallarotti, G.M. 1991. The limits of international organization: systematic failure in the management of international relations. International Organization, 45.

Garvin, D.A. 1993. Building a learning organization. Harvard Business Review, Jul–Aug.

Haas, E.B. 1990. When knowledge is power: three models of change in international organizations. University of California Press, Berkeley, CA, USA.

Haas, P.M.; Haas, E.B. 1995. Learning to learn: improving international governance. Global Governance, 1995.

Heckscher, C.; Donnellon, A., ed. 1994. The post-bureaucratic organization: new perspectives on organizational change. Sage, Thousand Oaks, CA, USA.

Levitt, B.; March, J.G. 1988. Organizational learning. American Review of Sociology, 14.

Risse, T. In press. Let's argue: persuasion and deliberation in international relations. International Organization.

Zacher, M.W. 1999. The United Nations and global commerce. Department of Public Information, United Nations, New York, NY, USA.

MANAGEMENT AND NETWORKS

Brown, L.D. 1993. Development bridging organizations and strategic management for social change. Advances in Strategic Management, 9.

Gray, B.; Wood, D. 1991. Collaborative alliances: moving from practice to theory. Journal of Applied Behavioral Science, 27.

Hardy, C.; Phillips, N. 1998. Strategies of engagement: lessons from the critical examination of collaboration and conflict in an interorganizational domain. Organization Science, 9.

Johnston, R.; Lawrence, P. 1988. Beyond vertical integration: the rise of the value-adding partnership. Harvard Business Review.

Jones, C.; Hesterly, W.S.; Borgatti, S.P. 1999. A general theory of network governance: exchange conditions and social mechanisms. Academy of Management Review, 22.

Lawson, C.; Lorenz, E. 1999. Collective learning, tacit knowledge and regional innovative capacity. Regional Studies, 33.

Scott, J. 1991. Social network analysis: a handbook. Sage Publications, London, UK.

KNOWLEDGE MANAGEMENT

Argyris, C. 1977. Organizational learning and management information systems. Accounting, Organizations and Society, 2(2).

Davenport, T.H.; Prusak, L. 1998. Working knowledge: how organizations manage what they know. Harvard Business School Press, Cambridge, MA, USA.

Drucker, P.F. 1988. The coming of the new organization. Harvard Business Review, Jan–Feb.

Gore, C. 1999. Knowledge management: the way forward. Total Quality Management, 10.

Hedberg, B. 1981. How organizations learn and unlearn. In Nystrom, P.; Starbuck, W., ed., Handbook of organizational design. Oxford University Press, New York, NY, USA.

Huber, G.P. 1991. Organizational learning: the contributing processes and the literatures. Organization Science, 2(1).

Kahler, M. In press. Information networks and global politics. In Engel, C.; Keller, K.H., ed., Understanding the impact of global networks on local social, political and cultural values. Nomos, Baden-Baden, Germany.

Nonaka, I.; Takeuchi, H. 1995. The knowledge-creating company. Oxford University Press, Oxford, UK.

Senge, P.M. 1990. The fifth discipline: the art and practice of the learning organization. Doubleday, New York, NY, USA.

Stewart, T.A. 1997. Intellectual capital: the new wealth of organizations. Currency/Doubleday.

CIVIL SOCIETY AND GOVERNANCE

Clark, A.M.; Friedman, E.J.; Hochstetler, K. 1998. The sovereign limits of global civil society: a comparison of NGO participation in UN world conferences on the environment, human rights, and women. World Politics, 51.

Conca, K. 1995. Greening the United Nations: environmental organizations and the UN system. Third World Quarterly, 16.

Donini, A. 1995. The bureaucracy and the free spirits: stagnation and innovation in the relation between the UN and NGOs. Third World Quarterly, 16.

Hobe, S. 1997. Global challenges to statehood: the increasingly important role of nongovernmental organizations. Indiana Journal of Global Legal Studies, 5.

Judge, A.J.N. 1995. NGOs and civil society: some realities and distortions. Transnational Associations, 1995.

Keck, M.E.; Sikkink, K. 1998. Activists beyond borders: advocacy networks in international politics. Cornell University Press, Ithaca, NY, USA.

Najam, A. 1996. Understanding the third sector: revisiting the prince, the merchant, and the citizen. Nonprofit Management and Leadership, 7.

O'Brien, R.O.; Goetz, A.M.; Scholte, J.A.; Williams, M., ed. 2000. Contesting global governance. Cambridge University Press, Cambridge, UK.

Paul, J.A. 1999. NGO access at the UN. Global Policy Forum, New York, NY, USA.

Price, R. 1998. Reversing the gun sights: transnational civil society targets land mines. International Organization, 52.

Princen, T.; Finger, M.; Manno, J. 1995. Nongovernmental organizations in world environmental politics. International Environmental Affairs, 7.

Ritchie, C. 1994. The relation between the state and NGOs. Transnational Associations, 4.

Simmons, P.J. 1998. Learning to live with NGOs. Foreign Policy, Summer.

Spiro, P.J. 1995. New global communities: nongovernmental organizations in international decision-making institutions. Washington Quarterly, 18.

THE PRIVATE SECTOR AND TRANSNATIONAL RELATIONS

Butler, N. 2000. Companies in international relations. Survival, 42.

Conference Board, The. 1999. Global corporate ethics practices: a developing consensus. The Conference Board, New York, NY, USA.

Haufler, V. 2000. International business self-regulation: the intersection of private and public interests. Brookings Institution Press, Washington, DC, USA.

Hocking, B.; McGuire, S. 1999. Triangulating diplomacy: firms, NGOs and governments in the international arena. Paper presented at the 40th Annual Convention of the International Studies Association, Washington, DC, USA, Feb 1999.

Kogut, B. 1998. International business: the new bottom line. Foreign Policy, Spring.

Nelson, J. 1998. Building competitiveness in communities: how world class companies are creating shareholder value and societal value. The Prince of Wales Business Leaders Forum, London, UK.

Pauly, L.W.; Reich, S. 1997. National structures and multinational corporate behavior: enduring differences in the age of globalization. International Organization, 51(1).

Sikkink, K. 1986. Codes of conduct for transnational corporations: the case of the WHO/UNICEF Code. International Organization, 40.

Stopford, J. 1999. Think again: multinational corporations. Foreign Policy, Winter.

UNCTAD (United Nations Conference on Trade and Development). 1998. World investment report: foreign direct investment and the challenge of development. United Nations, New York, NY, USA.

Weidenbaum, M. 1993. The shifting roles of business and government in the world economy. Challenge, 36(1).

SOCIAL CAPITAL

Coleman, J. 1988. Social capital in the creation of human capital. American Journal of Sociology, 94.

Evans, P. 1995. Embedded autonomy: states and industrial transformation. Princeton University Press, Princeton, NJ, USA.

Foley, M.; Edwards, R. 1997. Escape from politics? Social theory and the social capital debate. American Behavioral Scientist, 40.

Fukuyama, F. 1995. Social capital and the global economy. Foreign Affairs, 74(5).

Granovetter, M. 1985. Economic action and social structure: the problem of embeddedness. American Journal of Sociology, 91.

Kawachi, I.; Kennedy, B.P.; Lochner, K. 1997. Long live community: social capital as public health. The American Prospect, 35.

Putnam, R.D. 1991. Bowling alone: America's declining social capital. The Journal of Democracy, 6(1).

PUBLICATIONS BY THE STAFF OF THE UN VISION PROJECT ON GLOBAL PUBLIC POLICY NETWORKS

Benner, T.; Reinicke, W.H. 1999. Politik im globalen Netz. Internationale Politik, 8.

Reinicke, W.H. 1998a. Global public policy. Foreign Affairs, 76(6).

———— 1998b. Global public policy: governing without government? Brookings Institution Press, Washington, DC, USA.

———— 1998c. Hands on the bridge. World Link, Jan–Feb.

———— 1998d. Policy cooperation in a post-interdependent world. *In* Bakker, A.F.P.; Gruijters, N., ed., Global order for sustainable growth. Emile van Lennep Memorial Conference. De Nederlandsche Bank, Amsterdam, Netherlands.

———— 1999a. Globale Ordnungpolitik: Gedanken zu einem überfälligen Thema. *In* Heilemann, U.; Kath, D.; Kloten, N., ed., Entgrenzung als Gestaltungsaufgabe: Festschrift zum 65. Geburtstag von Reimut Jochimsen. Duncker & Humboldt, Berlin, Germany.

———— 1999b. The other World Wide Web: global public policy networks. Foreign Policy, Winter.

———— 1999c. Trilateral networks of government, business, and civil society: the role of international organizations in global public policy. Pre-UNCTAD X Seminar on the Role of Competition Policy for Development in Globalizing World Markets, Geneva, Switzerland, 14–15 Jun 1999.

Reinicke, W.H.; Witte, J.M. 1999. Globalisierung, Souveränität und internationale Ordnungspolitik. *In* Busch, A.; Plümper, T., ed., Nationaler Staat und internationale Wirtschaft. Nomos, Baden-Baden, Germany.

———— In press. Interdependence, globalization and sovereignty: the role of non-binding international legal accords. *In* Shelton, D.H., ed., Commitment and compliance: the role of binding norms in the international legal system. Oxford University Press, Oxford, UK.

Reinicke, W.H.; Witte, J.M.; Benner, T. In press. Beyond multilateralism: global public policy networks. Internationale Politik und Gesellschaft.

THE AUTHORS, THE PUBLISHER, AND THE SPONSOR

Wolfgang H. Reinicke is Director of the UN Vision Project on Global Public Policy Networks, as well as being Senior Partner and Senior Economist in the Corporate Strategy Group of the World Bank. His areas of expertise include global economic integration and global public policy, global finance and development, international economic institutions, the political economy of ethnic conflict, transatlantic relations, and European integration. Dr Reinicke is a fellow of the World Economic Forum, a member of the Academic Council of the American Institute for Contemporary German Studies, and an adviser to several US and European foundations.

Before joining the World Bank in the spring of 1998, Dr Reinicke was a Senior Scholar at the Brookings Institution (1991–98), held positions as a strategic management consultant for Roland Berger in Munich and in the operations department at Dresdner Bank in London, and was a consultant to the National Academy of Sciences and the US Agency for International Development. He has published several books and many articles, been the recipient of numerous fellowships and awards, and held teaching appointments at several US universities.

Francis Mading Deng is Director of the UN Vision Project on Global Public Policy Networks. In addition to academic appointments in his home country of the Sudan and in several universities in the United States, Dr Deng served as Human Rights Officer in the United Nations Secretariat, as his country's Ambassador to Canada, the Scandinavian countries, and the United States of America, and as Minister of State for Foreign Affairs. In 1983, Ambassador Deng joined the Woodrow Wilson International Center for Scholars as a Guest Scholar and was subsequently nominated to be the Rockefeller Brothers Fund Distinguished Fellow. He returned to the Wilson Center as Senior Research Associate and was concurrently appointed a Jennings Randolph Distinguished Fellow at the United States Institute of Peace. In 1989, he joined the Brookings Institution as Senior Fellow, where he heads the African Studies branch of the Foreign Policy Studies program.

In 1992, Ambassador Deng was named Special Representative on internally displaced persons worldwide by UN Secretary-General Boutros Boutros-Ghali. For several years, he was a visiting lecturer at Yale Law School, where he gave seminars on law and nation-building in Africa. From 1996 to 1998, Dr Deng assumed the position of Acting Chair of the African Leadership Forum, during the imprisonment of General Olusegun Obasanjo, former Head of State of Nigeria and the founder of the Forum. Dr Deng has published many books and articles on Sudanese politics and society, internal displacement, and African politics, as well as several novels.

Jan Martin Witte is a Research Associate with the UN Vision Project on Global Public Policy Networks and a graduate student at Johns Hopkins School of Advanced International Studies in Washington, DC.

Thorsten Benner is a Research Associate with the UN Vision Project on Global Public Policy Networks and a Research Fellow with the German Society for Foreign Affairs, in Berlin.

Beth Whitaker is a Research Associate with the UN Vision Project on Global Public Policy Networks and a Senior Research Assistant at the Brookings Institution in Washington, DC.

John Gershman is a Research Associate with the UN Vision Project on Global Public Policy Networks and a visiting graduate student at the Woodrow Wilson School at Princeton University.

Contact information
UN Vision Project on Global Public Policy Networks
E-mail: gpp@globalpublicpolicy.net
URL: http://www.globalpublicpolicy.net

↜

Canada's **International Development Research Centre** (IDRC) is committed to building a sustainable and equitable world. IDRC funds developing-world researchers, thus enabling the people of the South to find their own solutions to their own problems. IDRC also maintains information networks and forges linkages that allow Canadians and their developing-world partners to benefit equally from a global sharing of knowledge. Through its actions, IDRC is helping others to help themselves.

IDRC Books publishes research results and scholarly studies on global and regional issues related to sustainable and equitable development. As a specialist in development literature, IDRC Books contributes to the body of knowledge on these issues to further the cause of global understanding and equity. IDRC publications are sold through its head office in Ottawa, Canada, as well as by IDRC's agents and distributors around the world. The full catalogue is available at http://www.idrc.ca/booktique/index_e.cfm.

↝

This study was funded by the **Better World Fund**, sister organization to the **United Nations Foundation**. The two organizations were established to support the goals and objectives of the United Nations, with special emphasis on the UN's work on behalf of economic, social, environmental, and humanitarian causes. This study was prepared as part of the UN Vision Project; this project aims to help strengthen the United Nations to act increasingly effectively and efficiently in this new and constantly changing environment in order to promote a more peaceful, prosperous, and just world.